CHANGE
ONE
THING

Change One Thing

Make one change and embrace
a happier, more successful you

Sue Hadfield

CAPSTONE
A Wiley Brand

© 2014 Sue Hadfield

Registered office
John Wiley and Sons Ltd, The Atrium, Southern Gate, Chichester, West Sussex, PO19 8SQ, United Kingdom

Library of Congress Cataloging-in-Publication Data is available

A catalogue record for this book is available from the British Library.

ISBN 978-0-857-08460-6 (pbk) ISBN 978-0-857-08458-3 (ebk)
ISBN 978-0-857-08457-6 (ebk)

Cover design by Mackerel Ltd

Set in 10/13 pt Helvetical LT Std-Light by Toppan Best-set Premedia Limited
Printed in Great Britain by TJ International Ltd, Padstow, Cornwall, UK

This book is dedicated to Elliot Eddy Hadfield, who is just beginning his journey.

Contents

5

INSPIRATION

What do other people do?
Page 93

6

PREPARATION

What can you do if you can't act now?
Page 119

7

IMPLEMENTATION

Finding the time
Page 137

8

DETERMINATION

Over to you
Page 163

"This is your time and it feels normal to you, but really, there is no normal. There is only change and resistance to it and then more change."

Meryl Streep

INTRODUCTION

You are living in interesting times

During your lifetime things have been changing constantly so that when you look back on your younger self you are amazed at the things that you now take for granted (mobile phones, the internet, wind turbines, cycle lanes, electric cars, barcodes, iPads, Amazon, Google, plasma TVs, men pushing baby buggies). There are also things that have disappeared: people smoking in restaurants, cinemas and on aeroplanes, metal dustbins, cheque books, many local pubs and small shops, Woolworths, Comet, videos, records and cameras with films.

And it's not just technology that has changed in your lifetime. Natural disasters, such as the "Boxing Day Tsunami" in 2004, Hurricane Katrina and the Pakistan earthquake in 2005 affect us all, for a while, as we become one world in the face of such destruction and devastation. Similarly, world events like the fall of the Berlin Wall (1989), the Channel Tunnel (1994), 9/11 (2001), the election of America's first black president (2008), even records being broken in the Olympics (and Murray winning Wimbledon), change the way that we see the world and consequently, the way that we see ourselves.

Your life will continue to change

We may welcome new gadgets in the belief that they make our lives easier, and we may regret the passing of the familiar things from our past, but the one certainty in life is that everything changes. Your personal life too will have changed: nobody stays the same person they were as a teenager. Can you remember a favourite book, or film, or band, or hobby, a person you admired, or your ambitions as a teenager? They would almost certainly be different to your choices today. The experiences you have had in your life have changed your attitude and will continue to do so.

1

You are leading an interesting life

In your life so far you will have passed through different phases. As a child you thought that you could be anything you wanted to be: if anyone asked, your answers might have varied from astronaut, to explorer, from vet to footballer, from author to musician. As a teenager, you probably felt confused and began to change or modify your aspirations. As a young adult, you may have begun to have doubts about whether you had chosen the right path. You will certainly have had some successes and relationships and achievements that make you feel proud of yourself. As your life progresses, it becomes complicated by relationships and ambition and social status.

Changes that have happened to you

Your life so far may not have been easy: you may have had accidents or illnesses, you may have been lied to or betrayed, you may have done things that you now regret. You may have found yourself doing things in order to fit in with others in your social circle or to make yourself feel secure in the future. Whatever resentment or sadness you feel about the past, it's over and only exists when you choose to recall it. There is no point in raging against the unfairness of life, or missed opportunities, or comparing yourself to those who seem to have it easy.

Changes that you choose to make

Many of the changes that have happened in your life have simply happened – you have had no choice in the matter. But you are not a helpless pawn in the game of your life; you have also made decisions that have changed the course of your life so far. When you make a change in your life, it can simply mean that you stop doing something that you have been doing (such as spending money on coffee everyday); or you stop doing something and replace it with something better (like cycling instead of driving to work); or you decide to add something new to your life (like volunteering).

If you have tried, but failed, to make changes in the past (such as when you made a New Year's Resolution), it may be because the goal that you set was too big or too general. Making a decision to "go on a diet" or to "take more exercise" is often doomed to failure because the ambition is too wide-ranging and open to disappointment. You may have had a feeling of hopelessness when things go wrong, but everything you have tried in the past is useful. You have not failed if you learn from your experiences and if you are determined to keep on trying.

Fear of change

You may have a sense of dissatisfaction or discontent with your life at the moment but feel anxious about making a decision that you may regret. It may seem safer to let things stay as they are and to settle for what you already have. You may unconsciously be waiting for something to happen that will cause you to make a change.

It takes courage to examine your life and to decide that there are things you would like to change, and it takes even more courage to do something about it. Research shows that when you are young you tend to worry about making a change because you are afraid that things might go wrong – that you might make the wrong decision. When, you get older, however, you tend to regret the things you didn't do (rather than the things you did).

We will do anything to avoid the feeling that we are taking a risk; we are afraid that we will not be able to handle the disappointment if it doesn't work out. We pack our lives with other things: moving house, decorating, dieting, buying more things – anything rather than make the change that we secretly want. But studies show that we tend to exaggerate our fears about things that could go wrong and anticipate that we will feel worse than we actually do. In fact, when we act on something we tend to accept the outcome: it is not doing the things that we would like to do that we regret.

Be proactive

Being proactive about your life (rather than reacting to things that happen) means examining what you are you are doing with your time and asking yourself whether this is the life that you want. Making the most of your life means investing some time and effort into thinking and planning and doing. It is your life and you are the person who can influence its outcome. A rich and fulfilling life usually includes job satisfaction and close personal relationships and these are interdependent. If you are not happy in your personal life, it is difficult to succeed at work; if you are unhappy at work, then you are likely to bring your misery home.

The changes that people want to make in their lives are usually connected to their relationships or their careers and the very idea of this can be daunting. The fears and doubts that accompany any such life-changing event can paralyze you into doing nothing. As you read this book, you will see examples of people who have faced similar fears, doubts and decisions and chosen to take their lives into their own hands and change things.

This book addresses the way that we avoid change and the reasons that we do this. It examines the way that you may have approached problems and decisions in your life in the past and will inspire and guide you to think about your life in the present. Doing nothing is also a decision: doing nothing means deciding to continue the way you are now; deliberately making a change in your life means making a decision that your life is going to turn out differently.

You may feel dissatisfied with your life at the moment but may not feel ready to make wholesale changes. But making **one** change in your life doesn't have to be daunting – even small changes can have a huge impact. Instead of feeding your fears and doubts by allowing them to dominate your thoughts, you can make the decision to embrace your desire to lead the best life that you can. When you decide to make a change, or to introduce something new into your life, you feel empowered and your life will never be the same again. Any small change that you make starts a positive cascade that affects all aspects of your life.

> But making **one** change in your life doesn't have to be daunting – even small changes can have a huge impact.

If you feel that your life is ready for you to make a change, for new ideas and challenges, this book will show you how to fulfil your ambitions. It will inspire you with the examples of other people, just like you, who want to achieve their dreams and live a life with no regrets.

Convinced? Just making *one change* in your lifestyle, however large or small, can alter the course of the rest of your life. Now read on and discover how to motivate and inspire yourself to take the steps you need to transform your life.

1

Motivation

You have your whole life ahead of you

"Millions who long for immortality don't even know what to do with themselves on a rainy Saturday afternoon."

Susan Ertz

"You have your whole life ahead of you. Don't waste it."

Did anyone ever say this to you when you were young? Have you ever said it to anyone else? Of course, it is true about all of us – ahead of us lies our future and it is up to us to spend however many years we have in the best way possible. The decisions we make about every aspect of our lives are not just taken at age 18 or 21 but throughout our lives.

Which do you want first – the good news or the bad news?
Well the good news is that of the people alive in Britain today, 10 million will live to be 100 (currently the number is 12,640). These people are called the Generation C (for centenarian) and it is estimated that three million of them are presently under the age of 16 and a further five and a half million are under the age of 50. Nine out of ten boys can now expect to live to reach the age of at least 65 (whereas, in 1901, life expectancy for men in this country was 45 and for women it was 49).

According to a 2011 report from the International Longevity Centre UK, with the support of Age UK, those who live until they are 100 tend to avoid specific cancers and have been able to resist certain diseases. So that those who do reach 100 "effectively avoid many of the conditions associated with old age".

There's plenty of time then. So what's the problem?
First of all, there isn't much time between the cradle and the grave. A new-born boy today can expect to live for 78.9 years and a girl to 82.9 (although it varies depending on where you live – a man living in Glasgow has 13.5 years fewer years than a man in Chelsea). You might think, "Well, I'm only 38 that gives me another 40 years to pursue my dreams". The trouble is that it doesn't work like that. The problem is that the increase in life-expectancy has not been matched by an increase in "healthy life-expectancy".

9

What age would you be happy with?

Anyone under the age of 65 will have benefited from a lifetime of free National Health Service care. Medical advances in our lifetime have improved mortality rates from heart disease and strokes and have made us aware of the dangers of smoking and drinking too much alcohol.

We are more aware of healthy eating and we live in a more affluent economy, with a consequent rise in living standards: people live in more comfortable, often central-heated, homes and are likely to work in safe and air-conditioned work places. So we should be living longer, but we don't just want extra years – we want extra active and healthy years.

Health Survey

Half of all Britons in a survey by Benenden Healthcare said that anything over the age of 83 would be a bonus. Out of 2,000 people, the researchers found that one in six said they would be happy to live until they were 70, while only a quarter had any desire to live to be 100.

Seven out of ten admitted they believed that the way they were living their lives would have an impact on their quality of life as they grew old. Four out of ten thought their diet would cause problems for them at a later date and a quarter thought they would suffer because of the amount of alcohol they presently consumed. Lack of exercise was also a big worry. Six out of ten said that they would rather die than be left alone in old age or be a burden to others because of infirmity and illness.

What does healthy life-expectancy mean?

So we want to live as long as possible, but we want to be in good health. Healthy life-expectancy is an estimate of the number of healthy years (free from disease or disability – like cancer, dementia or severe arthritis) that a person born in a particular year can expect to live. The average number of years spent with some kind of debilitating illness is subtracted from the average life-expectancy to give us "health-adjusted life-expectancy".

So what do you guess is the average healthy lifespan for the UK? (Write it down.) Once you know this age, try asking other people you know. Their guesstimates will vary wildly (in my experience from 40 to 80 years). People tend to guess based on the health of their relatives, or sometimes just because they know one person who has lived an active life to a great age: "Well, my aunt is 93 and she still does her own shopping and cooking."

Remember, like lifespan, healthy lifespan is an *average* age for the whole of the UK (including Glasgow). It does not mean that you will begin to suffer from an illness or disability at this age (and, indeed, everyone you ask will decide that the figure doesn't apply to them). So what do you think it is?

The average man in this country can expect to enjoy good health until he is 63 and the average woman 65, according to a report by the Office for National Statistics in 2011.

So, although life-expectancy has increased and our bodies are living longer, this doesn't necessarily mean that we will be leading the kind of active, adventurous life that we might hope for as we get older. As you read these figures, you, like everyone else, will be saying to yourself, "Well, that's the average. It's not going to be me. I'm determined to stay fit and well and lead a fulfilling life right to the end."

(If you want to know where to live: Monaco has the highest life-expectancy in the world at an average of 89.7 years. Chad has the lowest level of life-expectancy at 48.7 years. The United Kingdom comes in 30th at 80.2 years, while America ranks 51st in the table with 78.5 years. Japan has the greatest proportion of over-90s, followed by Sweden, Italy and France.)

Scientists at Johns Hopkins University in Baltimore conducted a study of 6,200 men and women over a period of eight years and isolated four habits that are the most likely to help you to have a long but healthy lifestyle. They said that not smoking made the biggest difference, followed by a Mediterranean-style diet (vegetables, fruit, whole grains and fish), regular exercise, and keeping a normal weight.

"Be happy while you're living, for you're a long time dead."

Scottish proverb

Of course, you don't just want to live healthily – you want those years to be happy and rewarding. You want to be able to look back on your life and know that you have fulfilled your potential; that you haven't wasted it in an unhappy relationship or a job that bores you. Indeed, you want to be aware that you are living a life worth living while you are living it – to know that you are learning new things and using your talents and abilities to the full.

If you think of people you admire, they are usually people with a passion: people who have discovered what they enjoy doing and then perfected their sport or their craft and pursued it to its limits. For most people, this is not easy to do. We all have the same things holding us back: that little voice telling us that we're not good enough; the family background that makes us conform; the tendency to laziness that stops us from achieving our potential.

It is easy to make excuses and to compare your lot in life unfavourably with others. It is true that many people who have made a success of their lives have done so with the help of a comfortable background and family support. It is, however, equally true that many of our heroes have come from humble backgrounds and have achieved their success almost despite their family upbringing or difficulties.

"Don't be afraid your life will end: be afraid it will never begin."

Grace Hansen

It is, of course, easier if you know what you want to do with your life from a young age. We watch the young Olympic athletes like Jessica Ennis and Tom Daley and know we can never be like them because they realized right from the start what they wanted to do and they were given the support and encouragement to fulfil their dreams. But all the support in the world wouldn't have made them champions without their own dogged determination and desire to win. We often forget this when we see them sail across the finishing line: the 5am starts, the strict diet, limited social life, the denial of pleasurably activities with their friends and families. All we see is the result: the modest smile to the camera; the self-deprecating comments; the cup held triumphantly aloft.

"Just don't give up trying to do what you really want to do. Where there is love and inspiration, I don't think you can go wrong."

Ella Fitzgerald

Is it too late?
It is true that there are some things that have to be started when you are very young if you are going to excel: it takes a

young body to be the best in some sports. It is possible, though, to do almost anything you want – whatever your age. You may not be able to become an Olympic champion, but it is certainly possible to decide on something that you want to achieve and to become good at it. For some sports and many creative areas of life, there are no age limits – you can become an artist, or an author, or a musician, or a traveller, or a canoeist, a marathon runner or an entrepreneur – whatever you want and whatever your age.

It is not just these kinds of creative activities that can be taken up later in life, many people have changed career and done something totally different in their 40s, 50s and even 60s and 70s. It is sometimes because of a life-changing event, like being made redundant, or having a baby, that makes people realize that they no longer want to do what may have suited them quite well when they were younger.

In fact, lots of people fulfil themselves *only* as they get older. They may not become famous because they just get on with it: studying for a degree in their 70s, setting up a business in retirement, writing a first novel, travelling around the world, becoming a good photographer, a keen birdwatcher, learning a new language, taking up horse-riding, singing or learning to play a musical instrument.

You may feel that you have been held back because of a difficult start in life, or poor schooling, or the lack of direction and support from friends and family. Almost all these things can also be a motivation – if you are able to put the past behind you and decide that it is never too late you can still, with a great deal of determination, and some planning, fulfil your dreams.

"Age is an issue of mind over matter. If you don't mind, it doesn't matter."

Mark Twain – who wrote The Adventures of Huckleberry Finn, *aged 50*

Some people who have succeeded late in life

Authors

- Mary Wesley wrote her first novel for adults when she was 70.
- Jean Rhys wrote *Wide Sargasso Sea* in 1966 at the age of 76 (after a lapse of almost 30 years).
- Laura Ingalls Wilder was 65 when she started *Little House on The Prairie*.
- Flora Thompson wrote *Lark Rise to Candleford* when she was 63.
- Raymond Chandler was 51 when he wrote his first novel, *Big Sleep*.
- Marina Lewycka wrote her first novel, *A Short History of Tractors in Ukrainian*, when she was 58.
- British doctor, Peter Roget, produced *Roget's Thesaurus* when he was 73.

Politicians

- At the age of 70, Golda Meir became the fourth prime minister of Israel.
- Ronald Reagan became president of USA just before his 70th birthday.
- Nelson Mandela became president of South Africa in 1994 when he was 74.
- Stanley Baldwin became chancellor in 1922 at the age of 55 and prime minister the following year. He resigned when he was 70.
- Lloyd George was 53 when he became prime minister in 1916.
- Churchill became prime minister for the first time when he was 65 and began his second premiership in 1951, when he was nearly 77.

Scientists

- Dorothy Hodgkin studied x-ray crystallography and was awarded a Nobel prize when she was 54.
- Lisa Meitner continued her atomic research into her 80s.
- Alexander Fleming discovered penicillin at the age of 47.
- Charles Darwin published his findings *On the Origin of Species* age 50.
- Barbara McClintock was awarded a Nobel prize when she was 81, for her discovery that genes can move within chromosomes.

Sport

- The oldest Olympic champion is Oscar Swahn, who won two gold medals in 1908 and 1912, and silver in 1920 at the age of 72 (for deer-shooting).

Music

- Verdi was 74 when he composed *Otello* and 80 when he composed *Falstaff*.
- Wagner was in his 60s when he wrote *Gotterdammerung*, *Tristan and Isolde*, and *Parsifal*.
- Beethoven was 53 when he wrote his ninth symphony.
- Susan Boyle won *Britain's Got Talent* at the age of 47.

Artists

- Michelangelo began *The Last Judgement* in the Sistine Chapel when he was 61 (and it took him five years to complete). He did not begin his work in St Peter's until he was 71.
- Titian painted *Diana and Actaeon* in his 70s.
- Tintoretto's work in the Scuola di San Rocco in Venice was done in his 50s and 60s.

- Rubens, Goya, Velazquez and Rembrandt were at their peak in their 50s.
- (You can see Toira Beck-Friedman's video of three octogenarian women artists by visiting: tbfstudio.com/a_portrait.html).

David Galenson, a professor at Chicago University, studied the ages of innovative artists considered geniuses in their field. He discovered there was no proven correlation between someone's age and being at the peak of their creativity. He divided all artists into two classes: Conceptualists – who, right from the start, have a clear idea of what they want to do – and Experimentalists – who develop slowly over a longer period and don't have such precise goals.

Conceptualist or Experimentalist?

It may be easier to follow your passion and develop your creativity when you are young, perhaps living at home, or with other young people. Students, who have a firm idea of what they want to be, often do well at school, because they have motivation and a clear goal. Being young usually means you have no real responsibilities to anyone else but yourself. Your overheads are virtually non-existent if you live at home – and minimal if you are a student or are single and living in a house share.

Being free of "grown-up" responsibilities no doubt gave Mark Zuckerberg the time to found Facebook at the age of 19, Tom Hadfield to create soccernet.com at the age of 12, and Nick D'Aloisio to develop an app called Summly while studying for his GCSEs (and sell it to Yahoo, in 2013, for £20 million). It is why all the young musicians, actors and sport stars, we see today are more easily able to follow their dream.

If you had no clear idea what you wanted to do when you were young, you may have found yourself studying for the wrong exams, the wrong degree, and then taking a job that wasn't really what you wanted to do. Sometimes, this is because of lack of self-confidence or direction; but it may be that you are simply a late-developer and that you didn't have the ability, facilities, or encouragement to do well when you were young.

Change one thing: your secret deadline

You may have given yourself an unspoken deadline: "I want to be working for a national newspaper by the time I'm 30" or "I want to be working for myself in the next three years". In fact, a poll of 1,000 40-year-olds by Skipton Building Society, in 2012, found that the average adult is as much as 19 years behind their own schedule with their life-goals.

This feeling of dissatisfaction is surprisingly common, not only in terms of career, but also in terms of the milestones that people want to reach in their personal lives and relationships. The research showed that most adults hoped to start a family by the age of 28 but that 38% are unlikely have done so 10 years later. Of those polled, most had hoped to have met their life partner by the age of 25, but 33% of them were still looking at the age of 40; 13% of them admitted they had yet to find a full-time job.

The targets that had been missed by a significant proportion of the people surveyed were: owning a car, writing a will, going abroad twice a year, getting married, or having a civil partnership, starting a pension, and – for 71% – earning more than £30,000 (which they had hoped to do by the time they were 31).

If you could go back in time and start all over again, what would you do differently? Would you still pursue the same career? If not, what do you now wish you could have been and done?

A study for the recruitment website, Monster.co.uk, revealed that 47% of adults in their 40s regretted not following their childhood dreams (compared with a third in their 60s). The report showed that the most common unfulfilled ambitions were being a doctor, a vet, a sports star or an actor. Those who gave these as their dreams had mostly ended up in education, or administration, or with a job in IT. Men seemed to be slightly more dissatisfied with their present jobs (44%) than women (40%).

When, however, they were asked what career they would like to pursue now, their aims had changed to the arts and entertainment industry, with one in 10 wishing they worked in broadcasting, film or music. A third of recent graduates also wished they had followed their childhood dreams, adding that they had become more realistic as they got older. One in six said they were now more focused on being happy rather than achieving money or fame.

The (perhaps secret) dreams that you may now have for yourself could well be very different from the ambitions that you had when you were young. You will have changed. Your life has moved on. You are not quite the same person that you were as a young man or woman with few cares or responsibilities. Your long-cherished dreams may have changed, perhaps because you realized that you didn't have the patience to be a doctor or that you didn't want the long hours of studying involved for many professions.

Sometimes, the changes that have happened to you will be because of outside events over which you have no control. You may have suffered illnesses, or your parents may have split up at a critical time in your education, or you may have had to move house, to a new area where you knew nobody. These kinds of experiences can affect your confidence, so that you feel reluctant to take risks or simply feel that you are not the kind of person who can follow your dreams and do what you would really like to do.

You may have realized the insecurity that accompanies many more apparently glamorous careers such as acting, or being a musician, or writer. As you get older, the importance of a steady income and regular working hours take on a new significance. You may be a whizz on the bass guitar, or hilarious as a stand-up comedian, but will it pay the rent? Perhaps you tried for a while and then gave up when instant success or critical acclaim didn't happen. Or it may be that you do still yearn for your childhood dreams, but somehow they have fallen by the wayside and you have found yourself following a different path.

Wanting it all
The prospect of trying to achieve everything can mean you achieve none of the things you most want. Many people rush headfirst down a career path they think will lead to money, status and success without considering the consequences to their personal lives. Sometimes, you just have to stand back and reflect. What do I really want in life? Who are the most important people in my life? Am I proud of my life so far? What could I do to improve it?

If you have a family, you will want them to thrive and to do well so your personal dreams and ambitions may have been pushed to one side. Having to juggle the often conflicting demands of modern life is stressful and sometimes, ironically, leads to the breakdown of family life that the paid work was intended to support.

> The status and financial rewards of any job are meaningless, if you are feeling constantly miserable and anxious.

The trouble is that, in the drive to "have it all", the most important things in life can slip to the bottom of the pile, as "wanting it all" comes to mean a relentless drive to earn more and buy more. We all know of relationships that have ended, children who long to spend more time with their parents, and friendships that are neglected, because work has taken precedence over the things that once mattered the most. The status and financial rewards of any job are meaningless, if you are feeling constantly miserable and anxious.

Quality time?

The UK has some of the longest working hours in Europe: the average working week is 43.5 hours (three hours longer than the European average). More than four million full-time workers work more than 48 hours a week and one in six works more than 60 hours a week, according to the TUC.

According to the Office of National Statistics, a typical working mother spends about 19 minutes a day with her children; working fathers spend even less. A UNICEF report in 2012 warned that British parents were caught in a "cycle of compulsive consumerism" – buying toys, gadgets and designer labels in an effort to compensate for the lack of quality time with their children. Their research showed that what children, and their parents, really wanted was more stable family time at home. The report also suggests that many women, who may have wanted children, find themselves childless because they have delayed motherhood until it is too late because of financial pressures or career ambitions.

The problem is, if you are a late-starter, by the time you have a clear idea of what you would really like to do with your life you may already have commitments and rent and bills and all the trappings of modern life. Once you have started on a life-path that takes you on a certain course, it is much more difficult to decide that you have made a mistake and to change track. This often causes a great deal of inner torment as it is difficult to balance duty and rationality with the realization that you have made a mistake and that there is something else that you would rather do.

It is common then to feel a sense of failure if you are a "late-developer" and if your life is not going the way that you had hoped it would. The overwhelming feeling when you have a general dissatisfaction with your life is one of helplessness: a feeling that this is your lot in life and you just have to get on with it. The result is that you do nothing and life continues as before.

It's your choice

It is, of course, much easier to ignore these niggling doubts and to put up with a life that isn't quite the dream, or even particularly happy. It can be frightening to move out of your "comfort zone" because, by definition, this is a reassuring place to be. The alternative is not necessarily doing something frightening or risky, just doing something you long to do, but which you feel you "shouldn't" because it doesn't conform to what people expect you to do.

You may feel trapped in a job that you hate, with colleagues you don't particularly like, because it is well paid, or at least pays the bills. Some people spend their lives making money, in order to lead a better life, and often sacrifice their health and their relationships in the process. Quite often, they then spend their later years trying to recover their health (belatedly joining a gym, "detoxing", having therapy) or patching up their relationship with their children.

Whatever age you are now and wherever you are in terms of career, or relationships, or family, you have the rest of your life ahead of you. Don't squander them by letting the days go by, doing things you don't enjoy with people you don't want to be with. These are the best years of your life and it is possible to make a living doing something you enjoy, to spend more time with people you like and to live a happy and fulfilled life. Lots of people do it and there has never been a better time to start.

> Whatever age you are now and wherever you are in terms of career, or relationships, or family, you have the rest of your life ahead of you.

2

Identification

Know yourself and what you want

"The best way of preparing for death is to make sure you have a good life. This doesn't mean you should live each day as if it were your last. You don't want to spend every day of your life with 18 anxious relatives around your bed and a priest warming up in the hall."

From *Never Hit a Jellyfish with a Spade*

Guy Browning

"Live every day as if it were your last" is just about the worst axiom to live your life by. The implication is that we should not waste any time doing things we don't enjoy, but should spend every minute in pleasurable activities (so, presumably, we would spend all day eating chocolates and having sex). This might be fun, but – for most of us – it's not practicable. Immediate gratification (such as eating a box of chocolates or drinking a bottle of wine), repeated often enough, is bound to have a long-term deleterious effect. And, because it's not your last day, you'll probably regret it.

We do, of course, have to do things in the short term that may not be pleasurable (like studying for an exam, or going to the gym) in order to benefit later. Delayed gratification means keeping going through boring or difficult times because you have an end-goal in sight. The trouble is that the goal often becomes obscured by the myriad events in life. So the long hours you were working in order to save for a deposit become routine; or the job you were doing as a stop-gap after university becomes permanent. But you keep doing it because you are afraid there is no alternative.

> "Too many of us are not living our dreams because we are living our fears."
>
> *Les Brown*

The treadmill

Leading a busy life can mean that you lose sight of why you are doing things. You don't stop to think, because there isn't time. The treadmill goes on relentlessly and it is difficult to step off and stand back and wonder where you are going. You

> Leading a busy life can mean that you lose sight of why you are doing things.

do things because you have to and there seems to be less and less time to do things because you want to.

When work dominates your life and you don't have time to do the things you want to do, the solution is often to take a holiday. The trouble is that this solves nothing; there's no point being unhappy, the rest of the time, for the sake of a few weeks in paradise. Getting more "balance" in your life becomes a mantra as you try to pack more pleasure into every spare moment.

The idea of having a "work/life" balance implies that the purpose of work is just to provide the means to get on with your "real life": the things you really want to do. Whereas the ideal for most people would be to merge the two so that your work and "life" are not separate but your whole life is spent doing what you believe in and want to do. To lead a truly happy life, we need purpose and challenge (as well as pleasure) and in order to discover what this is for you, you first need to check your own attitudes and values.

> "Success is not the key to happiness. Happiness is the key to success. If you love what you are doing you will be successful."
>
> *Albert Schweitzer*

In order to know whether you are successful, you have to know what your goals are in life and what you value the most. The word "success" is usually associated with financial gain and status or your place in the hierarchy at work. But your benchmark of success is unique to you, and when you define your own values and goals you are able to strive for a sense of satisfaction and happiness that comes from accomplishing what you really want to do. Schweitzer's "If you love what you are doing you will be successful" is true if your idea of success is having a sense of achievement, a sense of purpose, and a feeling of being fulfilled in your daily life.

Change one thing:
live in the moment

This sense of fulfilment can be achieved by "living in the moment". Which means, while acknowledging your negative feelings about past events, you focus on the present and what you are doing now. In his book, *Flow*, Mihaly Csikszentmihalyi, a professor of psychology, describes how the best way to achieve happiness is to choose activities where you become totally absorbed (thus creating the mental state he calls "flow").

When you are totally absorbed in this way, it is impossible to feel negative or have all those chaotic thoughts racing through your head; time passes without you noticing and you will be so engrossed you don't notice discomfort like feeling cold or even hungry. Csikszentmihalyi claims that a mind that isn't occupied in this way will think negatively: "it will focus on . . . recent grudges or long-term frustration".

His definition of happiness is having an active sense of accomplishment and improvement (as opposed to pleasure, which is satisfying our basic desires). It requires effort and mental energy to achieve this state (so it is not the same as watching television or any other kind of passive entertainment).

Csikszentmihalyi named nine different elements that are needed to achieve a state of "flow":

- Clear goals.
- Immediate feedback.
- A balance between challenge and skill.
- A merge of action and awareness.
- No distractions.
- No fear of failure.
- No feeling of self-consciousness.
- The sense of time is distorted.
- It is done for its own sake (rather than to make money).

Think about times when you have felt like this. What were you doing? What work can you do that would make you feel like this?

Feeling successful and being happy is a combination of being involved in work that truly absorbs you and at the same time being fulfilled in your personal life. For most of us, doing work we really want to do is only half of the story and we have to somehow find a way to also have time for our families and the important people in our lives.

Often, it is not until people reach the end of their lives that they begin to realize they have wasted a lot of time on things that weren't important. You, however, don't have to wait until then: take time to consider your own mortality and examine your life as if the time you have left is precious and you want to make the most of it.

Learning from the regrets of others, and making sure that you have no regrets as you get old, is possible – by choosing to live your life in the best way you can: the life **you** want to lead and not one that others expect of you. It's not easy, though: you have to be brave to analyse your life; decide if it's the one you want; and, if not, take the steps to improve it. Sometimes it takes a wake-up call in the form of illness or bereavement. But you can just decide right now that you are going to make the first step towards making a change to improve your life.

TED talk
In a moving TED talk, "Three things I learned while my plane crashed", Ric Elias explains his thoughts in the few minutes of silence after the engines cut and he heard the pilot say "Brace for impact".

"It all changes in an instant. We have a bucket list of all these things we want to do in life: all the friends I wanted to see, all the experiences I wanted to have."

He said that he no longer wanted to postpone anything in life. He regretted the time he wasted on things that did not matter, rather than people who did matter. He said since that day he has never argued with his wife, "I no longer try to be right. I choose to be happy". Above all, he said that he realized that the only thing that really mattered was to be a great Dad. (The plane actually landed safely on the Hudson River, New York).

Ric Elias said it was a gift to be able to see into the future but then come back and have the chance to live differently. You don't have to have a near-death experience to learn things about yourself that you would like to change.

9/11
Do you remember those poignant last phone calls that people made from the plane that crashed into the Twin Towers in 2001? Who would you ring? What would you say? Do you spend the most time with the people you are closest to? Do you ever say the words you would say if it were your last phone

call? Don't wait for a crisis to realize what really matters to you in life. Think about what you value and who you care deeply about.

Why not give them a ring now?

Before he died of cancer in June 2013, the author Iain Banks wrote thank-you letters to all his favourite authors and told them how much he had enjoyed and valued their books. If there are people in your life who have enriched your life, but who you have never really thanked, try writing them a letter.

Why not write it now?

Change one thing:
check your values

You probably haven't given much specific thought to your values. But everyone has a set of values, whether they are consciously aware of them or not. You may not have sat down and worked out what they are; you just have a sense of what is right and wrong, the way things "ought" to be and the way people "should" behave. Your values will have been affected by your family values and by those of the wider society that you live in. It is useful, however, if you have decided to make some changes in your life, to take some time to think about your current values.

"Think only on those things that are in line with your principles and can bear the light of day. The content of your character is your choice. Day by day, what you choose, what you think and what you do is who you become. Your integrity is your destiny . . . It is the light that guides your way."

Heraclitus

> The sociologist, Morris Massey, has described the three main periods in our lives when we develop our values. The first is the "imprint" period from birth to the age of 7. During this time, we blindly accept everything and learn to differentiate right from wrong.
>
> The age of 8 to 13 is called the "modelling" period, when we copy other people, mainly parents. From 13 to 21 is the "socialization" period, when we are most influenced by our peer-group. In this age-group, we often deliberately try to escape earlier influences in order to develop as an individual. Our values are confirmed by associating with people with similar views and aspects of the media that reflects this peer-group.

Your values affect the way that you live your life. They can change, and will certainly alter in order of priority, throughout your life, but ultimately they are the way you measure whether your life is going the way that you want it to. When the work that you are doing matches your personal principles, then it is likely you will enjoy it. When your "spare" time and the time spent with your family and friends reflects your values and ideals then you will feel good about yourself and will usually be content.

"When I do good, I feel good; when I do bad, I feel bad, and that is my religion."

Abraham Lincoln

If, however, you feel that you are always being compromised, for example if you work for a company whose ethos doesn't match your values (perhaps in the way it rewards, or looks after, its employees), then you will be constantly frustrated and unhappy. You may have had financial security as a priority in the past and so have been driven to relentlessly pursue promotion. The competitive atmosphere (that you may once have enjoyed) might not now match the person you have become. Your perspective on life has changed and so your values have changed (it may be you are now more financially secure) and you long for a harmonious, stress-free environment.

> "What is necessary to change a person is to change his awareness of himself."
>
> *Abraham Maslow*

Sometimes, it is when people have a break from work, either on holiday or because of illness, that they realize that they can't face the thought of going back. This often happens to parents returning to work after time spent at home on maternity or paternity leave. Suddenly all the things you used to value have been turned upside down and you don't want to work long hours in a stressful job. Your priority becomes your family – and getting a good night's sleep. You may feel guilty about this. You think that you should carry on as you always have done and ignore the fact that something momentous has happened in your life, which has turned your previous values upside down.

Similarly, if your values include social justice, equality, and respect for all people, regardless of age, nationality or religion, then you would not be happy living in a country whose government did not champion these views. You can identify the values of a country, or at least its government, if you look at the reasons that they give for awarding honours and medals (such as OBEs and CBEs) and it is interesting to observe how these have changed over the years in this country.

"Those who have little interest in spirituality shouldn't think that human inner values don't apply to you. The inner peace of an alert and calm mind is the source of real happiness and good health. Our human intelligence tells us which of our emotions are positive and helpful and which are damaging and to be restrained or avoided."

Facebook page of the Dalai Lama XIV 12/7/2012

Acknowledging that your values have changed (and may change again) can help you make decisions about what you want out of life. Instead of struggling in a job that you no longer enjoy, feeling guilty that you are not "up to it" any more, it may be better to reassess and make some choices about your values and priorities. You may decide to "downshift" or go part-time, or even embark on something completely different.

One of the reasons people give for moving out of the city to the country (and sometimes to another country) is that they want to bring their children up with the "old-fashioned" values that they believe they will find there. And if you look at the reasons people give for separating or divorcing, it is often because a gulf has appeared in the values of the couple that was not apparent when they first got together. Arguments about money, or children, or how to spend leisure time are usually caused by their differing values in these areas.

Spendthrift or cheapskate?

For example, if you are a spendthrift, then you enjoy money for the thrill of spending it. You get immediate gratification from the purchasing power of money and, although this may be short-lived, you can repeat the thrill by endlessly buying. The pleasure that you get from buying things often has nothing to do with need; you just enjoy the intoxicating feeling. This lasts for about 90 seconds after making a purchase and so has to be repeated to stop the feeling of regret that often follows.

"When I shop, the world gets better, and the world is better, but then it's not, and I need to do it again."

Confessions of a Shopaholic *by Sophie Kinsella*

A spendthrift will justify these purchases by saying that they deserve them, or they needed cheering up, or that they are presents for other people. They can be self-righteous about their attitude towards money: "It's only money", and believe themselves to be generous, and those who criticize to be misers or tightwads.

On the other hand, if you have ever been labelled a "cheap-skate", it may be that you believe money is hard-earned and not to be squandered in a frivolous manner. If it gives you more pleasure to save than it does to spend, then you will be annoyed by any extravagant or unnecessary purchases by your partner. Both these attitudes towards money might not be a problem, or even apparent, when you are single and deal with your own finances. But when these two differing values towards money merge in a relationship, conflict will inevitable arise – whatever your financial circumstances.

What can you do?
If you are in (or about to embark upon) a relationship, and one of you is a spender and the other a saver, then it is vital to be open about your attitude towards money and to be honest about your financial affairs. Shared values are often the reason why some couples stay happily together, despite appearing to be very different. If you know a couple where one of them is gregarious but the other is quiet, you may have said, "Oh, it's because opposites attract". But it is much more likely to be that, despite these differences of personality, *they share the same values*.

Sometimes, because we don't consciously think or talk about values, you can be attracted to someone who appears to share the same taste in things, or lifestyle, as you. You move in together, and it may not be until something happens – like one of you losing a job, or getting pregnant – that you realize that, in fact, you have different values. And so the arguments begin. For some people, this process is repeated over and over again, with different people, without them ever realizing what is fundamentally wrong about the kind of person they choose.

Dating websites are becoming increasingly popular in the UK, with more than 5.7 million people registered in September 2012, according to internet market research company comScore.

A recent study, by Chicago University psychologists, of 20,000 people who had married between 2005 and 2012, revealed that those who had met online were 25% less likely to divorce or separate than those who had met by chance. Just over a third of those surveyed had met their spouses using internet dating sites, and their answers showed that they were happier than those who had met at work, in a bar, or on a blind date.

The researchers said the results could be because of the sheer number of potential partners available online, but they could also be because they were required to share more information about themselves. Having to describe yourself, your interests, beliefs and values, right from the start of a relationship may be one of the reasons for marital bliss (although it is worth noting the report was commissioned by the online matchmaking company eHarmony).

Be honest about your values
An honest assessment of your ideals and principles will show you clearly why you may be feeling a sense of dissatisfaction

with your life. It may be useful at this point to jot down what comes immediately to mind when asked this question: What are your most important values – the ones that you try to live your life by? Thinking about behaviour of which you may approve (or disapprove) in other people can help. Try to write at least five that describe your values right now; you can add to the list as others occur to you.

> "People focus on role models; it is more effective to find anti-models – people you don't want to resemble when you grow up."
>
> *Nassim Nicholas Taleb*

If you are finding it difficult to define your values, it can be useful to think about recent times when you were happy. Try to identify what factors contributed to your happiness: who you were with; being outdoors; being engaged in an activity; or doing some good for someone else. It may also be helpful to think about what makes you feel proud of yourself: earning money; looking after your family; completing a project; being fit and active; or making something. You may then realize that what you value most in life are things to do with helping others, your personal development or having meaningful work.

Making a change in a significant area of your life, like your career or relationship, needs a lot of careful thought and preparation to make sure that you are giving yourself the chance of the best outcome. Taking time to identify your current values may not be easy and you will probably be tempted to skip the following exercise, but having a clear idea of what you value enables you to make good decisions about your future and the decisions you want to make.

With your own list, choose one word and then think of an example when you have demonstrated that this is one of your top values. Can you think of a time when this wasn't the case?

Of course, it is easy to think of virtuous words. It is like a job application form where they ask you for personal strengths. You can think of a wonderful word, that you are sure is true, but then comes the hard part: you have to find evidence to justify the word.

Let's imagine you have written the word **honesty** as one of your top values.

Try answering the following questions:

- Have you ever been charged too little in a shop or restaurant? What did you do?
- Are you always honest about your qualifications or experience on application forms?
- Have you ever exaggerated an insurance claim?

Try thinking of examples where you have (or haven't) demonstrated in the past few weeks each of the values on your list. This is the way that you can test whether they are true – or just wishful thinking. (You can also use this technique to check the authenticity of other people's declared values.)

When you have a short list of values that you are happy with, and that you feel reflect who you are, try putting them in descending order so that the top three are words that the people who know you the best would agree with (you could try asking them). With your values clearly established, you are in a much better place to make any potential life-changing decisions or even small changes in your life.

Keep the list of your values where you can access them easily – add to them and change them as things occur to you. The more options you have when making a decision, the more helpful it is to be able to refer to your values – ones that you have considered and know to be true. You may even want to compare your list with those of partners and friends. It could be an indication of compatibility.

"Nothing is at last sacred but the integrity of your own mind."

Ralph Waldo Emerson

What do you want out of life?
Life often proceeds at such a pace that we rarely spend time considering what we are doing and why we are doing it. Yet ask any parent what they want for their children and they will say, "I just want them to be happy", or, "I'd like them to find something fulfilling that they want to do with their lives", or, "I'd like them to achieve their potential", or, "I want them to have the opportunities I never had".

Parents seldom say that they want their child to become rich and famous. It is as if it is clear when looking at a child that their future happiness will come from having a life that is one of purpose and challenge. Whereas, for many adults, it seems that the idea of happiness is connected to money, fame and a life of pleasure.

> To lead a truly happy life we need to have purpose and challenge as well as pleasure.

To lead a truly happy life we need to have purpose and challenge as well as pleasure. Money and fame can provide pleasure in the form of instant gratification but, as many rich and famous people have found to their cost, it can ultimately be short-lived and unsatisfying without purpose and challenge in your life.

Regrets of the living

A survey of 2,000 adults by the British Heart Foundation, in 2012, found that more than half the people surveyed wished they had made a different choice in their lives, such as marrying someone different, living somewhere else, or following a different career path. Some 20% of the women surveyed regretted the time they had spent with the wrong partner (compared with 10% of men), although the most common cause of regret was not having travelled enough.

They found that, on average, we spend more than two hours a week thinking about things that we wish we had done differently. We typically have six things that we regret doing (or not doing), with lack of money being the main reason for not doing so (although 25% of those surveyed blamed their loved ones for holding them back, with a further 32% blaming their own lack of courage).

How many of these would be among your regrets? Which others would you add? Of the list on the next page, which ones could you still do something about? Are there any from your own list that are redeemable? The only one that can't be rectified is the last on the list: if someone you know has died and

The Top 10 Regrets

- Not travelling more and seeing more of the world
- Losing touch with friends
- Taking too little exercise
- Not saving more money
- Taking up smoking
- Being lazy at school
- Wrong choice of career
- Wasting years with the wrong partner
- Eating unhealthily
- Not asking grandparents more about their lives before they died

you have regrets about your relationship with them, the only thing you can do is make sure that you aren't repeating this behaviour with other people who are dear to you.

Change one thing:
prevent regret – act now

The remaining items on the list of regrets are all ones that you can do something about. If you recognize any as being something that you regret (or that may potentially be something you will regret), then you can decide now to do something about it. In the following chapters, we will examine how you can identify and change one thing that could transform your attitude towards life and make it one of joy and fulfilment.

Change one thing: no regrets

You can change the way that you look at life and decide to look at the things you regret in a different light. For example, "wasting years with the 'wrong' partner" can also be viewed in a different way. Whatever the relationship was like at the end, there will have been many occasions of pure happiness and contentment. Recall these and remember them instead of the bad times. You will have emerged from the relationship a little bruised and older and wiser and you will be able to put all you have learned into your new relationships. You will appreciate the aspects of your new partner that were absent in the last one. You will have become a better person because of your failed relationship and, it is hoped, you won't make the same mistakes again.

Or your *one* change may be that any regrets you have now you will use to change your behaviour in the future. So, if you have lost touch with friends, you need to think about why this happened and decide whether you would like to have them back in your life. Deciding that you would does not mean that they necessarily will be open to a renewed friendship. But it's worth a try. It's almost impossible these days for someone to disappear without trace and comparatively easy to track someone down. Alternatively, you may decide that this was a friendship that has run its course, but your sense of regret will have taught you something about how precious friendships can be and perhaps you will have learned to treasure the ones you now have.

Recognition

The need for purpose and meaning

"Your beliefs become your thoughts,

Your thoughts become your words,

Your words become your actions,

Your actions become your habits,

Your habits become your values,

Your values become your destiny."

Mahatma Gandhi

The American psychologist, Professor Abraham Maslow, undertook a study in the 1950s of successful and fulfilled people (including Abraham Lincoln, Albert Einstein and himself). His conclusion was that being successful and fulfilled was the natural state for all humans and we could all be effective and fully-accomplished in this way.

According to Maslow, once we have met our basic needs – food, water and sex, then shelter, safety and clothing – we can move on to our social needs and then to possessing self-esteem, before we finally progress to the ultimate goal of what Maslow called "self-actualization". This is the need for meaning and purpose in life – so that our work, our activities and our existence must be in line with our values and beliefs. Maslow said that this is the highest state that humans can achieve and that *it is possible for us all to achieve it.*

> "The specific form that these needs will take will of course vary greatly from person to person. In one individual it may take the form of the desire to be an ideal mother, in another it may be expressed athletically, and in still another it may be expressed in painting pictures or in inventions."

Abraham Maslow

Maslow identified 15 characteristics that people share who were identified as "self-actualizers". But he said it was not necessary to display them all. It has nothing to do with becoming perfect; it just means that you are fulfilling your potential – your values are matched by your effort, achievement and enjoyment.

The 15 characteristics
1. Acceptance of themselves and others
2. Highly creative
3. Able to tolerate uncertainty; perceptive about situations
4. Spontaneous in both actions and thoughts
5. Concerned for the welfare of others
6. Problem-centred (rather than self-centred)
7. Unusual sense of humour
8. Show a need for privacy
9. Ability to have peak experiences
10. Holds egalitarian beliefs
11. Accepting of other cultures but not deliberately unconventional
12. Strong sense of morality
13. Have meaningful relationships with a few people
14. Profound appreciation of basic experiences in life
15. Ability to be objective about things that happen in life

These, according to Maslow, are the characteristics of successful and fulfilled people. How many do you think describe you? Remember, it is not necessary to claim them all. Maslow believed that the reason people didn't have these characteristics was because their basic needs hadn't been met. He believed that living without these values would cause a self-actualizer to become depressed, cynical and alienated.

The need for meaning and purpose in life

The need for meaning and purpose is the pinnacle of what most of us want in life. The trouble is that we can spend our entire life stuck somewhere in the middle of Maslow's pyramid, constantly updating our home, food and clothing in order to feel that we belong and have a raised sense of self-esteem. The material things in life have become an end in themselves so that we spend our lives repeatedly moving house and doing home improvements; becoming obsessed with food and diets, restaurants and menus; and shopping endlessly for clothes and accessories (indeed, lots of wealthy and famous people do not seem to seek anything more).

Along the way, we may become part of a social group and develop good friends and a social life; if we're lucky, we may acquire a sense of self-esteem. But it's the next step – Maslow's "self-actualization", the feeling that life has a purpose – that we are searching for. When this is missing, it leaves you with a sense of dissatisfaction and a feeling that there must be more to life.

Maslow's model of the things that are present before we reach the pinnacle of self-fulfilment is a *description* of (mainly male) successful people – not a *prescription*. He doesn't mention needing a flat-screen TV, or a nice house with a garden, or a new car, or any of the trappings you think you need *first* before you can do the things you would like to do – the things that are your ultimate goals.

"Focusing your life solely on making a buck shows a certain poverty of ambition. It asks too little of yourself. Because it's only when you hitch your wagon to something larger than yourself that you realize your true potential."

Barack Obama

If you travel to other more "impoverished" countries, you will quickly become aware that people who live there are still capable of reaching the pinnacle of Maslow's triangle (such as love, a sense of community, and fulfilment in their lives). Maslow's hierarchy of needs is not universally applicable; it tends to reflect Western male middle-class values. If we look at people who have achieved "success" in terms of following their dream, despite their background or failures along the way, we can see that it is not vital to have everything in order first before we reach for our dreams.

People who made it anyway

- Van Gogh: Sold only one painting in his life and was often starving.

- Albert Einstein: Didn't speak until he was 4 and didn't read until he was 7. Expelled from school, his parents and teachers thought he was slow.

- Oprah Winfrey: Poor and abusive childhood. Sacked as a television reporter as "unfit for TV". She says: "I don't think of myself as a poor deprived ghetto girl who made good. I think of myself as somebody who from an early age knew I was responsible for myself, and I had to make good."

- Louisa May Alcott: Encouraged by her family to find work as a servant to make ends meet.

- Victor E. Frankl: Austrian psychologist who developed his approach to therapy while in a concentration camp. He said: "Live as if you were living a second time, and as though you had acted wrongly the first time."

☐ Stephen King: When his father walked out on his mother, when he was 2, they lived off handouts from relatives. His first book *Carrie* received 30 rejections and was retrieved by his wife from the rubbish.

💰 Madam C.J. Walker: Born into a family of ex-slaves and farmers and widowed at the age of 20. Started a cosmetics business and became America's first self-made female millionaire. She said: "I had to make my own living and opportunity! But I made it! Don't sit down and wait for the opportunities to come. Get up and make them."

☐ Maya Angelou: American poet, author and actress, became mute for five years after being raped by her mother's boyfriend at the age of 8. She says: "One isn't necessarily born with courage, but one is born with potential. Without courage, we cannot practise any other virtue with consistency. We can't be kind, true, merciful, generous, or honest."

🎬 Michael Caine: Brought up in near poverty; he was born with rickets. His mother was a charlady; his father was a gambler and a drinker who spent any money they did have at the bookmakers or the pub. Their home was demolished in the Blitz.

Many famous musicians and pop singers come from humble backgrounds. They didn't try to sort out their material needs first. They just got on with producing their music and enjoying themselves. They didn't let criticism (or the fact that other people were doing the same thing) stop them. Famously, even the Beatles were told by the first recording company they approached, "We don't like your sound, and guitar music is on the way out".

Having all your needs met, and your social life in order, is not necessary for you to do something fulfilling and purposeful with your life. It does, however, take motivation, determination and, perhaps, a willingness to give up the material comforts that you may take for granted.

Following a dream

The online publishing firm that Jenny worked for was losing money and wanted to make five members of staff redundant. Jenny was single and lived alone. She belonged to an amateur dramatic society and had always secretly dreamed of becoming an actress. She knew how financially insecure this would be, but decided to take the redundancy and at least have a try at making a living doing what she wanted to do.

First, she moved out of her flat and took a room in a shared house. Next, she emailed everyone she knew and told them of her decision and asked them if they wanted a cleaner; she explained that this might be sporadic if she did get work. That was nine years ago and she now makes a living acting with a Brighton company, called the Maydays, doing voice-overs, teaching improvisation (and some cleaning).

Jenny says that, at first, she was dismayed by the threat of redundancy and that the one change she made was to see it as opportunity and decide what she really wanted to do with her life. Once she had made that change, everything else was simply a matter of working out how she could make her dream come true. She says she has never been happier.

Change one thing:
see setbacks as opportunities

To avoid disappointment, people often seem to learn to not let themselves dream, or want, what they think they will be unable to achieve. They resign themselves to jobs they don't really enjoy; they say they are being "realistic" because they are trying to protect themselves from the distress that they think they will suffer if they don't get what they want. But being "realistic" often means just allowing your fears to drown out your dreams so that what you profess to want doesn't match what, deep down, you would really like to do with your life.

"The great danger for most of us is not that our aim is too high and we miss it, but that it is too low and we reach it."

Michelangelo

Regret

If you look back on your life, can you think of anything that you have done that you have regretted? What about things that you haven't done, opportunities that you haven't taken? One of the reasons people give for not making any big changes in their lives is the fear that they will regret their decision later. We often make completely irrational decisions based on the fear of regret. So, for example, you might stay in the same job rather than apply for promotion in a different town because you are afraid that it won't work out and you won't be happy in a different town.

In his book, *If Only*, Nick Roese says that when you make a decision and it turns out to be the wrong one, you will quickly get over it. He says that once you have acted on a decision you just accept it, whereas it is when you *fail to act* that you are filled with regret. In other words, not doing something – out of fear of the consequences – has the exact consequence you have been trying to avoid; it can make you unhappy for years afterwards. In fact, failing to take the steps that you would like to could mean living unhappily with your lack of decision for the rest of your life.

> failing to take the steps that you would like to could mean living unhappily with your lack of decision for the rest of your life.

Change one thing:
don't delay your life

Delayed life is when you know there are things you want to do but you always find reasons for putting them off. You may find yourself thinking that what is going on in your life at the moment is unusual, that when things settle down you will be able to think and plan more clearly.

It may be that one of your parents is ill, or your child is having a difficult time at school, or you have been asked to increase your workload. You think to yourself, "When this is over then I will turn my attention to . . ." or "I will work out how I am going to . . .". You postpone your dreams for some never-to-arrive time in the future when everything will be straightforward and there will be nothing to hold you back.

The trouble is, for many people, this time never comes. Life is always going to be full of mishaps and messiness – that's life. The trick is to judge when your life is just too full (when you have a baby, after a bereavement, or when you are ill) to contemplate the future and when you are using the normal ups and downs of life as an excuse. Truly difficult times lead to sleepless nights and emotional and physical exhaustion: the worst time to make any life-changing decisions. But waiting until your life is running smoothly could well mean waiting until it is too late.

For example, if you are struggling to make a decision you may find yourself saying things like:

"I can't do it until I inherit."

or

"I can't do it until I lose weight."

or

"I can't do it until the mortgage is paid off."

or

"I can't do it until the children leave home."

or

"I can't do it until I get a better job."

Every time you hear yourself beginning a sentence with, "As soon as . . ." just pause and think about what you are saying. The myth behind this way of thinking is that if you can just sort out these external things in your life then your inner life – your sense of joy and fulfilment – will be easier to achieve. In reality, happiness does not depend on getting what you want in a material sense. If you think you would be happier if you had a bigger house, or a new car, or designer clothes, try to think what you would want once you got these things. Would there always be more things to add to the list?

"One day Alice came to a fork in the road and saw the Cheshire cat in a tree.

'Which road do I take?' she asked.

His response was a question: 'Where do you want to go?'

'I don't know.' Alice answered.

'Then,' said the cat, 'it doesn't much matter.'"

Lewis Carroll

We often have to do things we don't want to do in order to get to where we want to be. But, too often, what starts as a short-term fix becomes a way of life; we lose focus and forget where we are going. If you are working at something you don't enjoy, make sure you are clear about the purpose – your ultimate goal. Do you really have a long-term plan? Or are you just using excuses because you are afraid of the changes you would have to make to live the life you would really like?

> Every time you hear yourself beginning a sentence with, "As soon as. . ." just pause and think about what you are saying.

The consequence of living a "delayed" life, or simply having the feeling that you are just working to pay the bills and to keep your "head above water", is that you feel increasingly stressed and anxious about life. You adopt a victim-like mindset: feeling that your life is beyond your control – an unending struggle to maintain your energy levels and a normal home life.

A successful life needn't be one where you are relentlessly climbing a ladder, never quite reaching the top. It can simply mean fulfilling your own potential. Your working life doesn't have to fit the pattern of a traditional hierarchical path of a higher salary and a better title. You can decide to take a different

> A successful life can simply mean fulfilling your own potential.

approach to success – one where you view your life as a whole and give your relationships and your creative self an opportunity to flourish and succeed.

Stress

A survey of 2,000 Britons, aged 18–65, about levels of stress (by Benenden Healthcare, published in 2011) revealed that arguments in families, caused by stress, led the average couple to fall out four times a week – over-spending, not helping enough around the home, and not having enough money to pay the bills being the main triggers. A quarter of them said that they had "gone days" without talking to their partner. And more than half described this as a "vicious cycle".

Two-thirds said they experienced the most stress at work, while a third said they felt under the most pressure at home. Six out of ten of those surveyed said that the stress had affected their relationship with their children and caused a slump in their performance at work. Four out of ten stated that Monday was their most stressful day and that they felt anxious at least four times a day. The main causes of stress at work were heavy workloads, the nature of the job, and tight deadlines – causing one in five to have time off work on at least six occasions in the previous year.

The causes of most stress

According to the survey, the following were the main causes of stress to couples:

- Work
- Finances
- Not getting enough sleep
- Their figure
- Commuting
- Diet
- Children
- Lack of sex
- Partner
- Lack of help around the house

The surprising result of the survey was that, despite half of them saying they had felt unable to cope with the stress they were suffering, 78% of those had never sought professional advice. And more than one in five said that they never talked to anyone about the stress that they were under. Many said that they turned to alcohol to forget their worries; a quarter said they just turned on the television; and another quarter said they often ended up having a rant at someone.

When you see the result of surveys like this, it seems obvious that the way many of us deal with stress actually only adds to the problem. Alcohol not only makes some people aggressive, and more likely to enjoy an argument, it also inhibits a good night's sleep and adds empty calories to your diet. Taking your frustrations out on your nearest and dearest is obviously not the ideal way to get rid of your pent-up dissatisfaction from your day at work.

Sitting in front of the television is the most common way people relax. But watching anything and everything night after night can make us lethargic and often mindless. Watching television blots out reality so that we don't have to face our thoughts and our problems. It's a way of escaping reality and keeping our thoughts focused on something outside ourselves. The trouble is that by preventing meaningful conversation, watching television (or playing computer games) can be counterproductive if we want to relax: the more we avoid thinking about life in the real world the more it makes us feel unsettled and anxious.

It is difficult to deal with work and home life separately, as each affects the other. When the source of stress in your life is related to relationship problems in the home, it seems obvious that the best course of action for all concerned is to work on the problems in an open and honest way. It must be the priority in your life. Everyone is affected by the breakdown of a family, from the children to the grandparents and to the extended family.

Being happy in a relationship where each person is equally fulfilled is something most of us would like for ourselves and for our children. All families go through difficult times: coping with moods and hormones, and different wants and needs, is all part of living with other people. Achieving

---

In his book, *Intimacy*, psychologist, Ziyad Marar, examines the four ingredients that are needed for true intimacy to take place. He says they are: kindness, heightened emotion, reciprocity and conspiracy (the feeling that you are the only ones in the room). The most important of all is mutual knowledge: we must be honest with each other to have a successful, loving relationship.

compatibility is understanding that our lives ebb and flow; that it is sometimes impossible to have any kind of "work-life balance"; that events beyond our control will happen and send everything off kilter – that this is the reality of sharing our life with others.

Wanting what is the best for the other person is a good measure of a loving relationship – and if each person wants this it can hardly fail. It is when this is missing that things start to come apart and the family home becomes a place of conflict and unhappiness. Making the decision to do something about your situation, particularly where children are involved, is probably the most difficult change anyone makes in their life.

Change one thing:
seek professional advice

If this strikes a chord with you, then you need talk to your partner and may need to get professional help; spare no expense in trying to sort things out and repair the situation as soon as possible. When you dread arriving home after a day at work, then you know you are in trouble. Your home should be a place of sanctuary, love and kindness for each person who lives there. It is essential for your peace of mind and personal fulfilment to sort out any family problems. If you chose "family" or "relationships" as your top values in Chapter 2, then make them your top priority. Single people, of course, might also benefit from professional help about careers, relationships or money.

"You may delay but time will not and lost time is never found again."

Benjamin Franklin

Body clock

At the age of 30, Leah's long-term partner left her for another woman. They had been talking about starting a family. Leah was distraught at his betrayal, but also worried about ever having children. Then she met Ian, who was 12 years older, and quickly became pregnant. They got married and soon had another child. Leah was happy to have a family, but disappointed by Ian's attitude. He left the entire child rearing up to her and also expected her to go back to work full-time. He was mean with his money and she had to pay for everything for the children from her wage.

Constant rows made Leah realize that she had been wrong to marry Ian, as her main aim had been to have children. She decided that as soon as her youngest had taken his GCSEs she would leave her partner. Then the firm Ian was working for went bankrupt and he lost his job with no redundancy. He became depressed and she knew he, at 60, would find it difficult to find another job.

Because they had always argued about money, they both found it difficult to accept the new situation with the financial power reversed. Leah found his constant presence in the house oppressive and they either argued or didn't communicate. She felt that it was her fault that she had married him and so felt responsible for his future.

Leah is like many women who panic because they can hear their body clock ticking and they want to have children. They rush into an unsuitable relationship in their 30s in order to have a family. But who can say whether Leah might have remained single and never had children and spent the rest of her life regretting that? Staying in the wrong relationship reflects your attitude towards yourself; only you can decide whether it is the right relationship and worth your time and effort to make it work.

Leah decided to wait until her children were older, but the atmosphere in the house made them very unhappy. When you have children, you have a duty to help them to feel secure and loved. Sadly, it is often the years when children are young that put the biggest strain on relationships because there is just so much to do. It takes a lot of talking and negotiating to make sure that the onus of childcare, domesticity and earning money is shared equitably.

The one change that Leah wishes she had made was to get professional help earlier in their marriage. Professional help is often seen as the last resort when a relationship is in trouble. But if there is any love left at all, it is worth the time and effort to salvage the relationship.

Children want their parents to stay together. But they grow up and leave and get on with their own lives and the parents are left behind. Sometimes, we use other people as an excuse for doing nothing because we don't want to take the responsibility for the decision – in case it is the wrong one. You can't blame other people for your own unhappiness; if you have decided what you want, what is most important to you, then it is your decision, your life.

Nobody should have to stay in a relationship that is abusive or harmful to mental health. But arguments about who does what and about money can be resolved if the will is there from each person. According to a study at Utah State University, the frequency of money disputes was the most reliable predictor of divorce: those who argue about their finances once a week are 30 times more likely to get divorced. The problem is that arguments about money in a relationship often arise because of different attitudes towards money, rather than because of the actual financial situation. In other words, it is not the amount of money available that causes the arguments: the wealthy are just as likely to row about money as anyone else.

Your position when you argue about money reflects your core values and so, if your values differ, it is difficult to find a compromise. What tends to happen is that beliefs become even more entrenched and an antagonistic attitude towards each other develops that becomes difficult to resolve. The trouble is that some people are reluctant to talk about money, particularly when they first get together, and so these issues never get sorted out until there is a problem, often because of redundancy or starting a family.

A survey conducted by American Express, in 2010, revealed that less than half of couples talked about money before marriage. The result of not disclosing your spending habits, or any debts you might have, is that things get out of control and may be beyond repair. Lying about how much has been spent and trying to hide credit card and bank statements are clear indications that there is a problem that needs sorting (whoever is doing the deceiving).

A report from the investment management website, Nutmeg.com, revealed that four out of ten women don't tell their partners how much they spend on clothes (reducing their spending by an average of £57.20 per shopping trip). Nearly one in three men covered up their spending on gadgets, such as mobile phones (reducing it by £94.04). Some deceived their partners by saying the item was in the sales when it wasn't; others said they hid their purchases, destroyed the receipts, and kept their bank statements secret.

Change one thing:
confront your debts

Whatever you have planned as your long-term goal, it is essential that you are truthful with yourself about how much you are spending and earning (and have an open and honest discussion about your finances, if you are in a relationship). You may need to sort out how you are going to pay off credit cards or student debt as you cannot embark on a new project if you have old debts hanging over you. Debt doesn't just go away because you blot it out of your mind (and thinking you might win the lottery is wishful thinking, not positive thinking). Ask yourself how big your debt has to be before you decide to do something about it.

> In a healthy relationship, having different earning power doesn't mean that you can't have an equal say in how the money is to be spent.

When discussing money with your partner, think about what would happen if one of you got made redundant, or fell ill, or became pregnant. Would you still demand that they pay half the bills? Equal partnerships are all about managing your differences and cooperating and supporting each other; with money, as with everything else, it can rarely be exactly 50:50. In a healthy relationship, having different earning power doesn't mean that you can't have an equal say in how the money is to be spent.

"How much money is enough? Just a little more than you have."

John D. Rockefeller

Change one thing:
admit you've made mistakes and move on

There is no point berating yourself about decisions that you made in the past. Don't waste your life wishing that you had taken a different career path; or not wasted so much time with a partner; or started saving earlier; or had children sooner (or later). All these things are in the past and you just have to accept that you may have made mistakes. You are not perfect; nobody is. Accepting that you've made a mistake in the past doesn't mean that you can't do anything about your life now. In fact, admitting that you have made a mistake is necessary before you can make a change.

"The curious paradox is that when I accept myself just as I am, then I can change."

Carl Rogers

Another reason that you may stay in unhappy situations is because once you have invested time (and probably money) in a decision, you are reluctant to admit you have made a mistake. You may have saved the money, had the big wedding, invited everyone you know, dismissed the doubts of your best friend or your parents, gone somewhere exotic on honeymoon, and then the doubts creep in (or even sometimes before the wedding). It is always difficult to know whether "pre-wedding nerves" are the instinct that you should be acting on – whether those early rows are just adjusting to living together or a sign of a turbulent future.

You deserve to be happy

We sometimes stay in situations that can literally make us ill. We persist in relationships that everyone else can see are unhealthy because we lose all perspective about life and what our values are. We do so out of fear of the unknown, the fear of making a mistake, the fear of regret. But mainly it is because of a lack of self-worth. We have a feeling that we don't deserve anything better than this life that we have fallen into – a feeling that we don't deserve to be happy and must pay the price for a decision that we made, perhaps many years earlier.

This isn't about walking away, just because the going has got tough (and it is always tough to work hard, and to care about each other, and to bring up children, and to take care of others and to be a useful member of society). It is about deciding to take charge of your life when all feelings of tenderness and even affection have vanished.

The rise in the number of divorces among those who expected to be enjoying the golden years of their retirement together, is a poignant reminder of the hopes and dreams that accompany the start of all relationships. Who knows how many years were wasted in hurtful arguments, bitter silences and mean behaviour before a decision was finally made. Facing up to unhappiness need not mean splitting up; if caught before too much damage is done, then relationships can be repaired and restored.

The effect of change on others

It's important to keep in mind that your desire to do something different with your life is likely to impact on others, whether it is your family, your friends or anyone else closely involved in your life. Sharing your goals – whether it is downsizing, or becoming self-employed, or even changing your diet and your lifestyle – is vital to your success.

But if you do decide to implement some changes in your life, some people aren't going to like it. It is you that wants to change, not your friends or your family. If you want to change and grow, then you have to be prepared to welcome their comments and to see them as an opportunity to learn new or different ways of doing things. An adverse reaction to criticism often means you are feeling insecure and defensive. Listen – but don't give up. It is your life and you are in charge of it; if you are not happy, those around you will suffer anyway.

> If you want to change and grow, then you have to be prepared to welcome their comments and to see them as an opportunity to learn new or different ways of doing things.

"Whatever course you decide upon, there is always someone to tell you that you are wrong . . . To map out a course of action and follow it to the end requires courage."

Ralph Waldo Emerson

Change one thing:
be honest with yourself and others

Making a purposeful change in your life often starts with examining in an open and honest way how you feel. It means being brave; it means being able to articulate what is wrong in an assertive way; it means assessing what is causing the stress in your life; and it may mean examining your attitude towards spending. It means being able to talk to others in an adult and civilized manner. It means acknowledging that things have gone wrong and that there needs to be a change to put them right.

"Any change, even a change for the better, is always accompanied by drawbacks and discomforts."

Arnold Bennett

Persevering through the difficult times means having a shared desire to want it to work, if you are in a relationship. It means making the change from only seeing the negative and moaning about that the things that are left undone to being appreciative and praising the things that are done. It is not easy to do this unless you are *both* willing to make the effort to change, and the only way to find this out is by communicating with each other calmly and effectively. Facing up to what another person really wants can be painful, but it is better than burying your head in the sand and just pretending that things are fine.

If reading this has made you feel uncomfortable, you will probably feel like closing the book and leaving it until a later date. The next chapter deals with our reluctance to face problems and offers strategies to deal with this. (If none of this applies to you, then you can breathe a sigh of relief and pat yourself on the back.)

"I'm not ready to improve my life.
I'm still in the complaining stage."

Procrastination

What's stopping you?

"Could we change our attitude, we should not only see life differently, but life itself would come to be different."

Katherine Mansfield

Is it possible to change?

Understanding that it is possible to change and to alter your attitudes and beliefs is an important part of the process. For example, the belief, in the past, that intelligence is fixed, led to the measuring of intelligence at 11 years of age: the eleven plus examination – with those "passing" going on to a more academic education than those who were deemed to have "failed". A child's potential was seen as fixed for life and, although there are examples of people who beat the system and still managed to fulfil their potential, there are many more whose prospects in life were limited by this belief.

Multiple intelligences

In 1985, Harvard professor, Dr Howard Gardner, developed the theory that we all have multiple intelligences (he suggested eight – including interpersonal intelligence, spatial intelligence and mathematical intelligence). His findings, and those of others working at the same time, showed that intelligence is not fixed at birth, but is growing and expanding throughout our lives. At any age and at any level of ability, we can continue to learn and to increase our intelligence.

Self-fulfilling prophecy

Believing that intelligence is static – you're either clever or you're not – then becomes a self-fulfilling prophecy. Once someone's intellectual abilities were measured and declared, then their possibilities in life narrowed: "I'll never be able to do that; I'm not clever enough". Therefore, the belief that intelligence is fixed has a profound influence, not only on the way that we educate our children, but also on our perceptions of ourselves and of our own abilities. As a comprehensive schoolteacher, I met many parents who believed that intelligence is fixed at birth (and that their children were never going to achieve academically). Passing on this attitude to their children limits their potential and curbs their enthusiasm for learning.

Do you avoid challenges?

Similarly, if you believe that it is impossible to change, you are more likely to avoid challenges in your life. Holding this belief means you will prefer to choose things that you find easy and, when faced with difficulties, you are more likely to give up. Interestingly, research on "gifted" children also indicates that they often don't achieve their early promise. One reason may be that if you have always found things easy and have been told that you are a genius, then putting in the effort to study is perceived as a sign of weakness.

Mindset

In her book, *Mindset: The New Psychology of Success*, Carol Dweck argues that having the idea that basic qualities, like intelligence, talent, or personality, are unchangeable leads to a "fixed mindset". She says that this causes stress and anxiety because people think that talent is all that is needed to be successful; people don't put the effort into things that they don't think they are very good at.

Whereas, having a "growth mindset" is a belief that any ability can be developed – it just takes hard work, motivation, commitment and perseverance. Any talent you appear to have is only the starting point. If you hold this view, you will love learning new things and have the resilience to accomplish what you want. Change is not a threat; it is something to be welcomed.

Change one thing:
replace envy with self-belief

A feeling of envy about other people's success indicates that you are not only feeling inadequate about your own abilities, but you also think you can't change. Those who believe that it is impossible to change are also more likely to be resistant to criticism and any kind of feedback or suggestions about how to improve (because, if you think you can't change, what's the point of listening?).

When you view other people as competition, their successes are seen as a blow to your self-esteem – as if there is only so much success to be had. This leads to a judgemental view of other people's success and constant anxiety about where you stand in the "pecking order". These feelings can consume you with bitterness and prevent you from moving forward – in other words, it reinforces your belief that you can't change.

Signs that you need to make a change in your life

Tick as many of the following that describe the way that you feel about your life:

- ☐ I get angry quite often
- ☐ I tend to blame other people when things go wrong
- ☐ I seek revenge when someone hurts my feelings
- ☐ I am impatient
- ☐ I usually have a feeling of helplessness when something goes wrong
- ☐ I can be obsessive about things
- ☐ My life seems to lack focus
- ☐ I find myself regularly envying other people
- ☐ I try to be in control
- ☐ I suffer from addictions
- ☐ I am a jealous person
- ☐ I seem to be in a constant state of limbo
- ☐ I get upset quite often
- ☐ I don't take criticism well
- ☐ I tend to judge other people's behaviour
- ☐ I suffer from fatigue
- ☐ I feel sorry for myself
- ☐ My life sometimes feels joyless
- ☐ I feel unappreciated
- ☐ I feel that life is passing me by
- ☐ Work dominates my life

If you have ticked six or more of these statements, you deserve credit for being so honest. More than ten ticks also indicates that you are feeling dissatisfied with your life and are ready to make a change. Choose one thing from the list that you would like to change and notice each time you think or behave in this way. By recognizing, and identifying it, you are making the first step to dealing with it.

Change one thing:
focus on the things you do well
and feel proud of them

Make a list of all positive attributes that you know
are true. Begin the list, "I am . . . (so you might put
"a loyal friend", "a caring son", "hardworking", "good fun",
"ambitious" or "reliable").

Jot down positive comments, appraisals and praise that you
receive and read through them when you are feeling anxious
or down.

Review the checklist occasionally to monitor how you feel
as you begin to change your life. Whenever those feelings
of self-doubt or inadequacy creep in, read your list out
loud to yourself.

Being open to the idea of change means believing that it is possible to reject ideas that we have held onto for a lifetime – that it is possible to learn new ways of thinking and new attitudes towards life. People who believe in the possibility of change are curious about life and have a desire to learn how to live it in the best way possible. They enjoy challenges and are more likely to find creative or different ways of solving problems.

> It is possible to learn new ways of thinking and new attitudes towards life.

Don't forget you have already changed

If you have kept a diary at any time in your life, it is always amusing to note how much you have changed (looking at old photographs can also help you to recall how you felt then). The things that obsessed you as a teenager: having a boyfriend or girlfriend; the restrictions of living at home with parents; your popularity with your friends and the burden of schoolwork. All can seem trivial to the person you are now. Even in the last five years, your attitude towards life will have changed because events have happened to change you.

Change one thing: reflect on the changes that have happened to you

Think of five major events in your life since you have become an adult (such as illness, accident, the death of a close relative or friend, or the birth of a child, success or failure). Can you remember how these events affected you at the time and the way that you have modified or changed your behaviour since?

Grief and loss can often change people so that when they emerge from their sorrow they are more empathic and considerate: their values and attitude towards life has changed significantly.

Success can also change people, so that they can become self-centred – although true fulfilment actually enables people to become more caring and compassionate. It is impossible to go through life without suffering, but it is also part of life to experience great joy and happiness. Nobody remains the same person after a traumatic or an amazing experience; we have to accept and learn from the things that happen to us.

> It is impossible to go through life without suffering, but it is also part of life to experience great joy and happiness.

Changes you have chosen

So, you may have been affected by events in the past that have caused you to change your outlook and attitude towards life, but you will also have made many life-changing decisions of your own volition. It is unlikely that you have had the same job all your life, or lived in the same house, or that your friends are the same ones you have always had. Even compared with a few years ago, the way you spend your spare time, your means of transport, the kind of food that you eat, the exercise you take, will probably be different.

> Nobody remains the same person after a traumatic or an amazing experience; we have to accept and learn from the things that happen to us.

Change one thing: welcome change

You have made these changes in your lifestyle because you have decided that what you were doing no longer suits you. You may have clung on to your old habits, or your old car, or your old girlfriend, for as long as possible because you don't like change. But, in the end, the pain of staying as you are outweighs the pain of changing – and then you change.

> But, in the end, the pain of staying as you are outweighs the pain of changing – and then you change.

"And the day came when the risk to remain tight in the bud was more painful than the risk it took to blossom."

Anais Nin

This is the reason that people often have to reach rock-bottom before they actually stop doing something (like drinking, smoking, eating unhealthily or being unhappy at work). Remembering changes that you have already made brings the realization that, although change is difficult, you have done it before – and this empowers you to do it again.

Research about the average British worker

Typical British workers have six different jobs over the course of their careers. They also have 10 job interviews, 12 pay rises, suffer redundancy or unemployment at least once and are late a total of 188 times in their lifetime. Over a third have a second job to make ends meet, and the average person has one office romance, and 125 days off sick (these last two were more likely if the work is in the culture or sports sector). A study of 2,000 workers showed that just a third were happy with their careers (www.OnePoll.com, March 2013, for Benenden Healthcare).

This research indicates that there are many people for whom work is more a source of pain and illness than a life-enhancing, rewarding experience. The researchers found that the average worker goes through a rough patch in their relationship at least twice because of work. The other negative effects of work-related stress were listed as: arguments, relationships ending, heavy weight-loss or weight-gain, tiredness, too much alcohol and missing quality time with their children. Three out of ten of those in the survey said the effect of work on their personal life had led to them seeking medical help.

The "end of history" illusion

Research by Dr. Daniel T Gilbert, a Harvard psychologist, and others, (published in the *Journal of Science* in January 2013), indicates how people underestimate the amount they will change in the future. They found that people were much better at recalling what they were like in the past than imagining how much they would change in the future – no matter how old they were.

They concluded that we tend to believe that we have reached the peak of our own personal evolution and, no matter how much we have changed in the past, we find it difficult to imagine that we are going to keep on changing in the future. The authors of the report called it "the end of history illusion" and said that the downside was that people made decisions in their youth (like getting a tattoo or getting married) that they sometimes came to regret.

"We always overestimate the change that will occur in the next two years and underestimate the change that will occur in the next 10. Don't let yourself be lulled into inaction."

Bill Gates

What are you afraid of?
The fear of change and the reaction of others can lead you to justify doing nothing: your job might be boring, but it pays the rent; you argue all the time with your partner, but it is better than being on your own; you dislike where you live, but it is safe and familiar. It can be daunting to examine your life and realize that you have been closing your eyes to the things that are wrong because to open them would mean confronting the possibility of change and the effort it takes to make that change happen.

Procrastination
Do you feel that the reason you have not changed the things in your life that are making you unhappy is that you are a

chronic procrastinator? For behaviour to be seen as procrastination, it must be counter-productive, needless and delaying. We usually feel guilty for procrastinating, and if it lasts over a period of time it may induce stress; often there is a secrecy – we don't tell others what it is we have hanging over us.

The accepted belief is that we procrastinate because of lack of willpower or ambition or, more probably, laziness. When we procrastinate, we are fully aware of what we are doing, but we suffer and feel bad because we are putting things off. The strange thing about procrastination is that we may actually want to do the very thing we are putting off and may instead do something that we don't particularly enjoy (like cleaning the kitchen floor or sorting out drawers).

Sometimes, this results in self-sabotage: have you ever left a job application until the last minute and then had to rush it to meet the deadline? Not filling in bureaucratic forms such as tax returns will mean that you have to pay a penalty, and yet procrastinators will leave it until the very last minute – or fail to do it in time.

A survey of 1,000 men and women by ecigarettedirect. co.uk claims that we procrastinate for an average of one hour and seventeen minutes every day. This works out to about nine hours a week or 19 days a year or 1.140 days over a lifetime.

The activities we are most keen to avoid until later are DIY, domestic chores (such as laundry, ironing and cleaning) and dealing with bills and household administration. Nine out of ten of those surveyed said they regularly put off tasks until the last possible moment. The most popular delaying tactics include having a cup of tea, a bite to eat, a cigarette or a toilet break.

Why do we procrastinate?

In his book, *The Procrastination Equation*, Piers Steel links procrastination with impulsiveness. So if you live for the moment, you will tend to favour activities that offer immediate gratification. You would rather do things where the result is immediate than things that have a long-term effect or take a long time to finish. He says that we think up strategies that are quite ingenious in the way they allow us to convince ourselves that we are really busy. Tasks such as watering plants or sorting out sock drawers become urgent priorities over less favoured – but more time-consuming or important – chores.

The good news

The good news, if you are a procrastinator, is that you will do it in the end. By definition, procrastinating only means putting off what you know you are going to end up doing. If we are talking about trivial things, procrastination can be a good thing. At least your kitchen floor will be clean and your sock drawer tidy. Positive procrastination can mean putting something off until tomorrow so that you can do something else today. This is good. You are still going to do it. Even this conscious realization can stop you procrastinating.

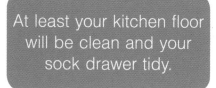
At least your kitchen floor will be clean and your sock drawer tidy.

But avoiding the big decisions in your life isn't procrastinating – it's avoidance; it's the "delayed life" concept we looked at in the last chapter. It can carry on through the whole of your life, so that you never do what you really want to do, or achieve your dreams, because you are waiting for a later date when you will feel certain and the time will be right.

"If you want to be certain, you should never get married. You should never change jobs. In fact, you might as well just stay home. Because I don't know anybody who is certain. That need to be certain is just procrastination."

Mark Burnett

Being afraid to make a decision can mean that you are afraid of failure – you want to be in control and to make everything perfect. You will never know what the outcome would have been if you had a made a different choice – you just have to trust that you have made the right decision at the time. Indecisive people can spend the whole of their life asking themselves, "What will happen if I do this . . .?" or "If only I was able to . . .". But once you get rid of the fear of making a mistake you are free to do what you know you want to do (and probably should have done years ago).

> But once you get rid of the fear of making a mistake you are free to do what you know you want to do.

"To live a great life, we must first lose our fear of being wrong."

Joseph Chilton Pearce

Perfectionism

Perfectionism can sometimes go hand in hand with the tendency to put things off. Perfectionists are driven to attempt an unattainable ideal and so always delay completion. A perfectionist sets impossibly high standards and then, if they do not reach their goals, they can become depressed. When faced with a number of choices, perfectionists find it difficult to operate because they are concerned about choosing the very best.

> "Perfectionism . . . will keep you cramped and insane your whole life . . . perfectionism is based on the obsessive belief that if you run carefully enough, hitting each stepping stone just right, you won't have to die."

Anne Lamott in her book on writing, Bird by Bird

Maximizers

According to researchers from Florida State University, there are two different types of decision-makers: "maximizers", who obsess about every choice they have to make, and "satisficers", who are happy with whatever decision they make.

The researchers say that the indecisiveness of maximizers means that they can cause themselves a great deal of unhappiness by being afraid to "commit" (in case there is something or someone better still out there).

Maximizers have to be certain that they have made exactly the right choice – which can be an exhausting task in a world with so much information freely available. So, for example, choosing a camera could become a time-consuming project: researching thoroughly, consulting everyone, and weighing up the options. In the end, even when a purchase is made, there will be a feeling of dissatisfaction because new information, or a new model, becomes available.

The researchers say that this tendency to analyse their choices, even after one has been made, can damage a maximizer's big life-decisions, such as buying a house, their love life and their careers.

> "Strive for excellence, not perfection."

H. Jackson Brown Jr

Case study

Mike gained six A-levels at school, because he wasn't sure what degree he wanted to take and was keeping his options open. At university, he studied Politics, Philosophy and Economics and began a career in the civil service. He worked long hours and in his first five years he changed the department he worked for three times. He frequently buys a new mobile phone, camera or electronic gadgets because he wants the latest model. He became involved in local politics, but failed to get elected to the council, and then his interest waned. Meanwhile, he had a few girlfriends, but would always walk away when things became serious.

You may know people like Mike. They are often dissatisfied with the career they have chosen and find it difficult to commit to any one person. Mike is a typical maximizer because, even after he has chosen his career, he is not happy; he thinks there is something more rewarding out there. He is a workaholic and never has time for satisfactory relationships, because he is not willing to commit himself to one person in case someone better comes along. He is often stressed, and his tendency to take on more and more responsibility at work is affecting his health.

Is it possible for Mike to change?
You already know the answer to this one. It is not possible for anyone to change Mike – only he can decide to do this. But if you recognize yourself as a maximizer, then you have the power to do something about it – if you want to. The first step, as always, is recognizing that it is a problem. The next step is deciding you want to change and the next one is doing something about it.

Every time you find yourself agonizing over a decision, ask yourself how big an effect it will have on your life. For food and most consumer products the effect is short lived – make your decision quickly. For things that have a lifelong impact, think about your values: instead of making choices based on pleasing your parents, or what other people might think, make sure they are *your* choices. It takes a lot of self-awareness to change something that has grown into a habit over a lifetime. But it is possible.

Only you can decide if you would like to change something in your life. Don't be afraid of tackling something that has been worrying you for some time: the unresolved problem that keeps you awake at night. The dilemma that causes you stress and drains your energy will also affect other areas of your life and solving this will have a positive cascading effect.

> It takes a lot of self-awareness to change something that has grown into a habit over a lifetime. But it is possible.

Learned helplessness

In his book, *Learned Optimism*, Martin Seligman explains how positive thinkers see any difficulties in their lives as being temporary and not their fault, whereas negative people view their problems as permanent and their own fault. Even when good things happen to people who tend to be pessimists, they see these events as being short-lived and do not expect their good fortune to affect other parts of their lives.

Seligman calls this "learned helplessness", meaning that they have become literally helpless in the face of what they see as insoluble problems. Perhaps because of experiences in their childhood, they have become resigned and passive about their lives. They are constantly anxious and, because they feel that nothing they do makes any difference, they have given up trying.

Change one thing: think positively

Seligman argues that it is possible to change this kind of passive, negative attitude to your life. You can learn to nurture your inner strengths and, if you are motivated and want to change, learn to develop a more positive outlook on life. You have to be prepared to challenge your old way of thinking and unhelpful beliefs. It is not easy to change a way of thinking that may have been developing throughout your life. But it is possible.

Procrastination can mean avoiding confrontation – particularly confrontation with ourselves. We do not want to face the fact that we are unhappy or that there are things about our lives that we wish were different. Admitting this to ourselves means taking the first step to doing something about it; admitting it to others is usually the second step, because it means articulating exactly what is wrong.

You can decide now to make that one change: begin by deciding that you are going to stop comparing yourself to others; their achievements don't diminish yours in any way. Don't fall into the negative-thinking trap: "I'll never be able to do it", or "I've never had any luck in my life", or "I'll never achieve what they have done" or "Other people had a better start in life".

Life is not school; your achievements aren't going to be ranked and pasted on a board. This is your decision about your life. Only you know what you would like to do with your life and only you can take the steps that you need make. Your future stretches out ahead of you and can be as bright as you want it to be.

Led by Professor Elaine Fox, a team of researchers into the science of optimism, at Essex University, have found that two forms of mental training significantly change the electrical activity in the brain. Greater activity on the right side of the brain is found in people who suffer from negativity, anxiety and pessimism, but when the training was carried out daily for seven weeks it was found that brain activity equalized: the mood of the participants lifted; they felt more optimistic and slept better.

The first activity was a meditation exercise involving sitting in a quiet place and focusing on a physical sensation like breathing. They suggested doing the exercise for 10 minutes initially then building up to 20 minutes. In the second exercise they were required to look at a screen which showed 15 angry or blank faces and 1 smiling face. Participants searched for the smiling face and clicked on it. Then the process is repeated with a new set so that you become quicker and quicker at spotting the happy faces. The idea is to train the brain to look for positive images so that your brain becomes more easily able to tune into positive thoughts.

You can try the exercise yourself at http://baldwinlab. mcgill.ca/labmaterials/materials_16fa_c_80BBC.html

"Never mind a book on how to improve myself. I need a book on how to improve everyone else in my life."

5

Inspiration

What do other people do?

"Often people attempt to live their lives backwards: they try to have more things, or more money, in order to do more of what they want so that they will be happier. The way it actually works is the reverse. You must first be who you really are then do what you need to do in order to have what you want."

Margaret Young, Simple Abundance

Do what you need to do

You already know what you would like to change in your life; you realize that it is possible and you recognize that you have made changes in your life before. We have looked at some of the likely reasons that you may have been putting things off. Remember that most people face the same hurdles: nobody finds it easy – they have the same insecurities and aversion to risk. Ask the people you know whom you admire; their lives will rarely have been one smooth transition to where they are now.

In this chapter, we will meet some people who decided to take their lives into their own hands and fulfil their dreams. You can be inspired by their successes and learn from those who made mistakes.

Buying a business

George studied sports science at university and got a job with a London council. Meanwhile, he bought a flat with his childhood sweetheart, Lizzie, who worked for a publishing firm in the city.

After a few years, George told Lizzie that he was getting bored with his job and that, in fact, he had a dream of becoming a butcher. He discovered that a local butcher in their home town wanted to sell his business. Lizzie was supportive and said that she had been hoping they were going to start a family, but realized that she would never be able to stay at home with a baby as long as they had the huge mortgage on their London flat.

George usually spent most Saturdays going to watch his home team play football; instead he now began working, for free, in a butcher's in their High Street.

Every time he went to visit his parents, he met with the local butcher and discussed buying him out. Still he was cautious and finally agreed with his girlfriend that they would move back to their home town and he would work in the butcher's for six months to make sure that the price was right and that he still wanted to do it.

What is remarkable about this story is that within the first year of ownership George had increased the turnover of the shop by 30%. Lizzie became pregnant and resigned from her London job. With the profit, George was able to employ more people so that he could take days off and be at home with his family.

Change one thing: if you are in a relationship, plan together

Like the other stories in this book, this is a true story and I have included it not because I think that there are thousands of people out there with a burning desire to be a butcher, but because I think their story shows how it is possible to fulfil your career dreams and still have a happy family life. Making one change (his Saturday football habit to volunteering in a butcher's) made George confident that he was making the right decision. Lizzie and George discussed their ideas, goals and plans, together, so it wasn't a case of one of them pursuing a dream at the expense of the other.

Hard work and determination

Notice also, however, how much hard work and determination went into putting the plan into action. Fulfilling your dreams of running your own business does not mean just talking about it, nor just making a plan, nor walking out on your job. It means careful research, perhaps volunteering, and saving furiously – paying out money on financial and legal advice, and making personal and financial sacrifices in the short term. It means discussing every step with your partner and making sure that you both share the same vision of the future. This needn't mean that you want exactly the same things in life. But it does mean that you share each other's values and one of those must be a desire to make each other happy. It's a tall order. But it is possible.

We have looked at all the possible reasons you have been putting things off; next you have to clarify your goal. At this stage, your goal may be a general one like: "work for myself", or "get out of this relationship" or "feel healthy". If you find yourself with a list of goals, then choose the one that will make the biggest difference to your life. Lots of people don't have one big goal, but several different ones – you can achieve them all – just tackle one at a time.

> If you find yourself with a list of goals, then choose the one that will make the biggest difference in your life

Ask yourself these questions:

- Am I living the kind of life I want?
- What kind of life do I want?
- Am I working towards this life?
- What steps do I need to take to achieve this? and (if you are in a relationship)
- What kind of life does my partner want?

Clarify your goal

The goal you set yourself should excite and motivate you. You have a vision of how your life could be as you work towards achieving it. Keeping your goal as your purpose and focus in life will stop you getting thrown off track or using all the excuses discussed in Chapter 4 to delay and procrastinate. Once you have clarified your goal you can begin to build a plan of action. Don't be in too much of a hurry to get to the end point: the success of your plan will depend upon your preparation, research and staying power.

It is important that you write down your goal, or your dream, or the kind of life you would like to lead (in whatever form – electronic or paper). Make sure that you can see it every day – there is little point in writing something down and then it disappearing into a folder on your computer or a page in your diary.

> Don't be in too much of a hurry to get to the end point: the success of your plan will depend upon your preparation, research and staying power.

Change one thing:
don't get stuck in the past

Another lesson to learn from this story is that it is possible to change track – from wherever you started out. As a schoolteacher, I saw numerous young people make their exam choices and degree choices without any real idea of what they wanted to be. The trouble is that people think that once they have made their choice that's it – there's no turning back – or even moving forward, in a different direction. You don't have to live your life honouring decisions that you made when you were 15 or 16.

The raising of the retirement age means that the idea of a career for life will become as rare as a job for life is these days. Changing track (if it is planned and well thought out) is not irresponsible; it is recognizing that times have changed and that you have changed as well. Keeping your body healthy and thinking positively about your life will extend your healthy lifespan so that you really can live life to the full and achieve everything you want to in the precious years ahead.

People who had a different job before they became famous:

- Postman – Russell Brand
- Mini-cab driver – Pierce Brosnan
- Glove cutter – Tom Jones
- Burger King employee, lifeguard, lift operator – Madonna
- Pavement artist – Robert Redford
- Cement mixer – Michael Caine
- Hospital porter – Mick Jagger
- Fish filletter – Annie Lennox
- Grave digger – Rod Stewart
- Social worker – Paul O'Grady
- Door-to-door insurance salesman – George Clooney
- Embalmer – Angelina Jolie
- Cook in a fire station – Jennifer Saunders
- Singing telegram – Sinead O'Connor
- Tarzan-o-gram – Chris Evans
- Hairdresser – Delia Smith, Whoopi Goldberg
- Trained to be a priest – Johnny Vegas
- Air stewardess – Melinda Messenger, Trisha Goddard
- Fire-eater in a circus – Bob Hoskins
- Lion cage cleaner – Clive James, Sylvester Stallone
- In a pop group – Melvyn Bragg, Damon Hill, Jeremy Irons

(from *Celebrity Lowdown: Incredible Facts and Lists About The Famous*, by Mitchell Symons)

And, of course, as we saw in Chapter 1, many people do not have one single dream that they cherish throughout their lives – and even if they did, that choice may no longer be an option. We tend to become focused on one particular path and fail to pause and consider whether it is the one we still choose to follow. Your perspective on life, and what you want out of it, changes as you develop and mature: the reasons that you made a particular decision in the past may no longer be valid. And the world changes, too. One of the reasons that George was able to buy the butcher's was because nobody in the butcher's family wanted to take it on. Anyone trying to make a living in a local shop, like a baker's, fishmonger's or greengrocer's, has to battle against the access and price that big supermarkets are able to offer.

> Your perspective on life, and what you want out of it, changes as you develop and mature: the reasons that you made a particular decision in the past may no longer be valid.

Minimize the risk: Test the market

Selling anything to today's well-informed consumers, with so many choices at their fingertips, means that you have to do even more research and analysis to make sure that you have something different to offer. To test the market, always start small, to minimize the risk. If you are hoping to sell your home-made cards, pet portraits, silver jewellery or hand-thrown pots, try craft markets or party plans in friends' houses before you rush into leasing a shop with all its overheads. Make sure that there is a need for your service or product before you start. Don't forget that selling on the internet works only if enough people know about your website.

Writing in *The Sunday Times* (21 April 2013), John Treharne, founder of the Gym Group, described how he set up his company after research showed that 70% of people only use the gym equipment at a health club. He set up his first no-frills gym in 2007, in Hounslow, for members paying £9.99 a month, and had 6,000 members before the doors had even opened. Today, he has 32 gyms across Britain and employs 98 staff. He told the paper, "If you are in it for the game, you will fail. Remember, you want to start and run a successful business. It's a lot of hard work but it can be so much fun."

"Why should we all use our creative power? Because there is nothing that makes people so generous, joyful, lively, bold and compassionate, so indifferent to fighting and the accumulation of objects and money."

Brenda Ueland

Observe or volunteer

On a careers course I used to teach (for adults who wanted to change career path), the students were required to volunteer, or observe, for a few days in the area that they were thinking about. They were always amazed at how easy it was to be accepted when they offered their services. In one class, I had different students at an estate agents, a florist, a vet's practice, riding stables, a gym, a driving school, a garden centre, a hospital and a few at different types of school. It takes some courage just to ring up and explain that you would like to work for free to find out if you would enjoy their line of work. But what's the worst that can happen?

In fact, all of the students found the experience invaluable (often because it made them realize that the job wasn't to their liking). Some of them enjoyed it so much that they tried numerous places – even things they had never considered until coming on the course. You don't have to be on a university course to do this – just decide how much commitment you are prepared to give before you ring. (George volunteered every Saturday for six weeks and in the end they paid him.)

Do the research

As well as volunteering, or observing, it is always a good idea to talk to other people who work in a similar area. You have to be quite astute, as some people will want to show off and tell you only how easy it is and how successful they have been. Others may have a jaundiced view (particularly if they are employees rather than owners) and try to put you off.

Draw up a set of questions before you go and, if possible, record or jot down their answers. Make sure that you ask them first for a convenient time and say that it won't take longer than 10 minutes.

Some questions you could ask:

☐ How long have you been doing this?
☐ Was it always a dream of yours?
☐ How did you get started?
☐ How much money did you need to start with?
☐ How much do you think you would need today?
☐ What do you enjoy about the job?
☐ Are there any downsides?
☐ Would you recommend it to me?
☐ What is your main competition?
☐ Are there any qualifications I should have?

A word of caution

If you do decide to give up a precious day off, or even part of your annual holiday, just be sure that you serve the time that you promised.

The first time you do a day volunteering it will be interesting, the second time you may find yourself left to your own devices, it will be the third and subsequent days that you will begin to see what the job really entails.

If you are resistant to the idea of working for free, then just try observing or shadowing someone whose job you would like.

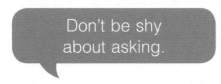
Don't be shy about asking.

Don't be shy about asking – it is better to find out if this is what you really want before you make any big decisions.

"No one lives long enough to learn everything they need to learn starting from scratch. To be successful, we absolutely, positively have to find people who have already paid the price to learn the things that we need to learn to achieve our goals."

Brian Tracy

Learn from the mistakes of others

Chris worked in insurance, but after inheriting some ornaments and furniture from an aunt he developed an interest in antiques. He began buying things at car-boot sales and then selling them at antique fairs. He also tried selling things on eBay and on his own website – although he found it tiresome to package delicate china and glass in order to post them. When a small shop, with accommodation upstairs, became vacant he decided to take the plunge and he sold his own two bedroom flat and took out a long lease.

He had an opening party one evening and was pleased to sell a few paintings. A few people called in to say how attractive the shop window always looked. After that, he spent day after day, sitting behind the counter, looking out at the world passing by. He missed the lively jokes and banter of his old office, but could not afford to employ an assistant because he was barely making enough for himself. The highlight of his day was closing the shop at lunchtime and walking to the pub across the road for a sandwich and a beer. He never dared to stay long in case he missed a sale. He persevered through a long and cold winter before finally giving up and selling at a loss.

Make a commitment

If Chris had done some research or volunteered in a shop first, he would have had some idea of what was involved. Remember, though, that offering to volunteer is a commitment; make sure that you are always professional; turn up on time; ring in sick only if you really are; ask lots of questions; be prepared to do the work nobody else wants to do.

You are there to learn and observe: you are unlikely to be given the most interesting or responsible jobs as a volunteer. But for thousands of people, volunteering (or being an unpaid intern) has been the way into the job of their dreams. At the very least, your placement could be the source of a good reference (if you work there long enough) and gives you a glimpse of the work involved.

> Be prepared to do the work nobody else wants to do.

Chris, however, didn't go back to his old job. He took a course in antique and furniture restoration and discovered a shared workshop where people brought in their items for him to restore. He still sells antiques online and at fairs, but realizes that working in isolation in a shop was very different to the life that he had imagined.

Volunteering in a charity shop for a few months (the change he wishes he had made) could have saved him a lot of heartache. Even imagining what his life would be like alone in a shop all day would have given him some insight and prevented an expensive mistake.

"But then, if one scheme of happiness fails, human nature turns to another; if the first calculation is wrong, we make a second better: we find comfort somewhere . . ."

Jane Austen, Mansfield Park

Match your talent and your interest to your values

Although Chris knew that he was interested in antiques, he hadn't realized how much he valued the company of other people and being part of a bigger organization. Just having a talent or a passion for something isn't enough to set yourself up in business unless you know yourself well enough to know that you can ride out the difficult times, the long hours and the periods of uncertainty, that most entrepreneurs face at the start.

So if, for example, you enjoy cooking, your dream may be to set up your own restaurant, but if you are not prepared for the long hours and inevitable consequences for your social life you might need to rethink. There are, however, other things you could do that might fulfil the same need. For example, in Brighton, there are a number of companies (such as CanTina, Cook for You and The Pudding Cow Chef) who offer to cook dinner parties in your own home.

"Ask yourself what you would do even if you were never paid. That's a clue to what you should be doing and, of course, finding a way to be paid for it."

Dr Joe Vitale

Change one thing:
examine your finances

Making the change from a secure PAYE-type job may mean making some sacrifices, but you will gain that feeling of motivation, excitement and enthusiasm that means you are living the life that you choose. Most people need to have money saved, another part-time job, or source of income, or a supportive partner to be in the position of being able to risk following their dream. Perhaps the biggest problem you have when making a change in your life is your relationship with money. Lack of money is one of the main reasons people give for not doing the things they want to do and not leading the life that they want to lead. It is true that to make a change in your life it is easier if you have enough money in the bank to make you feel secure about making that change, but it won't happen without some effort from you.

> you will gain that feeling of motivation, excitement and enthusiasm that means you are living the life that you choose.

Lots of people have good business ideas, but if start-up money is required and the banks won't lend it, they remain only as good ideas and never get off the ground. Some people remain in miserable relationships for the simple reason that they can't afford to move out and start again. Relationships might not break down in the first place if there were fewer rows about money and more time spent together.

> According to a YouGov survey in December 2012, commissioned by Relate (the relationship support charity), 59% of the 2,742 people polled said they were worried about their economic prospects in the future.
>
> Of those, six out of ten said they shared their fears and concerns with their partner and four in ten said they turned to other members of the family. One in ten said they wouldn't turn to anyone at all.
>
> Nearly one in three said that they argued more with their partner or family as a result of money worries; 55% of women worried about having enough money to cover the everyday costs of food, rent and household bills (compared with 49% of men).

If you want to figure out where your money goes, work out the minimum you need to spend each month to pay for your essential needs. Compare your income and basic expenditure and calculate how much you have left for non-essentials. The ideal is to spend no more than 50% of your income on essentials (shelter, heat and food) and then at least 20% on savings and pensions. This should leave 30% of your income for everything else or to save towards your change of lifestyle.

It's no good spending all this time working out how much you spend and what you can cut back on, if you then carry on as usual. You have to be vigilant about your spending if you want to have a healthy bank account and money saved up for your new venture. Try the Money Lover app (free on iPhone and Android), which sets up alerts and tracks your transactions. Or use an online budget-planner, such as the one on moneyadviceservice.org.uk, and keep it up to date.

Change one thing:
break small spending habits

Deciding to immediately stop small spending habits can make a big impact when it comes to living within your means or building up your savings for your future. If you buy just one lottery ticket every week, that's more than £100 a year and the average cost of daily and weekend newspapers is £400 a year.

Try TheDemotivator.co.uk, where you can type in anything you buy, its price, and how often you buy it. It then tells you its total cost to you over a lifetime (so, for example, buying a sandwich for lunch every working day for £3.50 would cost £875 a year and £39,355 over a lifetime). In fact, a survey by Officebroker.com discovered that the typical worker spends £7.81 a day on lunch, drinks and other snacks. They estimated that the total bill would be £88,971 over a lifetime.

(This works with weight-loss too: data from the Medical Research Council in Cambridge showed that halving the number of calories eaten at breakfast didn't cause people to eat any more during the day. Their overall intake was reduced by 270 calories a day – which is 98,550 calories a year. Even if you halve this estimate, it would mean losing at least a stone in weight. Similarly, instead of starting another diet, you could try changing just **one** thing like drinking water instead of soft drinks or alcohol. Set yourself a time limit of a month and see the effect – on your pocket – and on your waistline.)

According to a survey of 5,000 people by Scottish Widows, one in three in the UK has not saved a penny and a further third said they had less than £1,000 in savings. But a survey by Halifax bank, of people who saved, showed that women saved 41% of their annual salary (despite earning less), while men saved 23%: an average of £7,699 for men and £8,211 for women.

"He would die with nothing to reproach himself with, and under the impression that if only he had had the money he might really have lived and might even have achieved something great."

Søren Kierkegaard

Change one thing: start saving

If you have decided that money is the main reason you are not leading the life that you want to (in order to start a new business, or work part-time, or to be at home with your children, or to move) then you have to confront your spending and decide what is important to you and what makes you happy. It may be that you are spending too much in order to compensate for the discontent you feel

> It may be that you are spending too much in order to compensate for the discontent you feel doing a job that you don't enjoy.

doing a job that you don't enjoy or because you are in a relationship that doesn't make you happy. The prospect of breaking your spending habit may be daunting, but you have to delay gratification if you have decided you are going to achieve your goal.

Before you buy anything ask yourself:

- ☐ Do I need it?
- ☐ Can I afford it?
- ☐ Will I use it?
- ☐ Is it cheaper elsewhere?
- ☐ How many hours/days do I have to work to pay for it?
- ☐ Is it worth it?

Change one thing:
swap your shopping habit

If you want to introduce a new habit (like saving money), you have to get rid of your old habits.

- Instead of shopping, try doing something else in your spare time and always use cash instead of a debit or credit card.
- Use your local library instead of buying books and DVDs.
- Cancel your gym membership and walk more (use a skipping rope or hula hoop for low-cost exercise at home).
- Go to the supermarket less often (freeze what you don't need immediately), as you always buy things you don't need – or use smaller shops.

Less choice saves time and money. Discuss with others their money-saving tips.

"The chief cause of failure and unhappiness is trading what we want most for what we want at the moment."

Unknown

Change one thing:
boost your income

Increasing your income will boost your efforts to save money more quickly. This doesn't mean falling into the trap of working all hours, but taking on one-off work or doing overtime to bring in extra income can be enjoyable and motivating if you have a goal in mind. It might also be the time to ask for a promotion or a pay rise at work, if you feel that you deserve one. What's the worst that can happen?

Extra money without working

Try something you've never done before, like renting out a room – you can make £4,250 a year tax-free (spareroom.com) – or renting out space in your loft or basement as storage (storenextdoor.com). You can now rent out your bicycle or barbecue by the week (thesavvyearner.com) or your driveway (parkatmyhouse.com). Sell things you no longer use at car-boot sales or use sites like preloved.co.uk, where things are advertised by area so there is no need for postage.

> Try something you've never done before.

Once you start looking for ways to make money, it becomes easier to save because it makes you think twice about spending it (particularly when you begin to realize how much money you have wasted on things you have hardly used). Car-boot sales and charity shops are a good way of satiating your shopping habit if it is difficult to give up.

> Once you start looking for ways to make money, it becomes easier to save.

A portfolio career

Remember Jen in Chapter 3, who had a dream of acting, but still needs to keep on cleaning other people's houses to make sure she always has a regular income to pay the rent and bills? This is a fact of life for most people who decide to leave a conventional "9-to-5" job, with sick leave, a pension and paid holidays, to follow their dream. Sometimes it means doing more than one job, at least until your new career is established (and, of course, you have to be realistic about the likelihood of ever making a full-time income from writing, or painting, or photography, or music).

Most people in these kind of creative jobs have to do something else to support them (such as teaching), but being prepared to do this does mean that you still get to spend your life doing something you love. A portfolio career means you have to be well-organized and make sure that you don't end up sacrificing your passion by becoming over-committed and exhausted.

Having the experience and knowledge is only part of what is needed to escape from a routine job into more of a "lifestyle business". You have to be prepared to be versatile and to seize opportunities as they arise. Working for yourself is not a soft option – not having to turn out of bed for an employer doesn't mean you don't have to get up early and work long hours. The difference is you want to do it: you are motivated and in charge of your own life; you want to get out of bed because you are filled with a feeling of excitement and enthusiasm that money just can't buy.

> You want to get out of bed because you are filled with a feeling of excitement and enthusiasm that money just can't buy.

"The road to happiness lies in two simple principles; find what interests you and that you can do well, and put your whole soul into it – every bit of energy and ambition and natural ability you have."

John D. Rockefeller

So far, we have looked at the stories of some people who have decided to follow their dream and change their lives. We can see that just because you once enjoyed your job doesn't mean you have to stick with it for the rest of your life. Events like redundancy, birth, death and divorce can lead you to re-evaluate what you have been doing. But the decision to make a change can also come from within – from a growing sense of dissatisfaction or frustration. When your circumstances change they become trigger points that may make you ask, "Are my reasons for doing this job now the same as the ones when I started it? Is this really what I want to do now?"

> Just because you once enjoyed your job doesn't mean you have to stick with it for the rest of your life.

For all of the people in this book, the change they made in their lives was a process – making a radical change still means making that first step. Just make sure that you don't do anything too hasty: it's not about walking out on your job or your relationship – learn from the examples in this book, save some money and always have a plan.

Preparation

What can you do if you can't act now?

"The really happy person is one who can enjoy the scenery while on a detour."

Unknown

If you have commitments and duties to other people in your life, you may have a temporary goal that isn't quite your dream, but is realistically what you can achieve at the moment. The change that you can make may not be massive, but could still make a difference to your life and your future. For example, you may want to earn some money of your own, but also want to be at home with your children until they start school. Your goal is to be able to do something that allows you to do this.

> The change that you can make may not be massive, but could still make a difference to your life and your future.

When our children were small, we lived in a chalet in a remote part of Cornwall overlooking the sea. It was beautiful, but we were still paying a mortgage and bills on a house in Yorkshire that we couldn't sell. I spent every spare minute when our children were asleep marking GCSE and overseas exam papers. This wasn't exactly my ideal job, but I enjoyed the mental stimulation and it kept me in touch with my job as an English teacher. More importantly, it enabled me to contribute to the family finances and stopped us sinking into debt until I could return to work.

It is interesting to consider whether it is possible to achieve the kind of self-fulfilment that Maslow was suggesting if you are living in a family with young children. Of the 18 people that he used as exemplars for his theory, only a few were women (including Eleanor Roosevelt). One reason for this, of course, is that he was writing in the 1950s and using some historical figures as well as contemporary ones, and so it was always going to be more likely that men would be able to reach the pinnacle by becoming "all that they were capable of". Maslow didn't need to consider that, in an equal relationship, both partners may want to achieve this.

One or both parents often have to put their dream on hold while their children are small. But then Maslow said that self-fulfilment wasn't something you could achieve at a young age (he interviewed many undergraduates, but could find none that met the requirements of fulfilling their potential). If you feel that you are working towards the place you want to be and are motivated by doing the best for yourself (and your family), then you will feel positive about the possibilities for the future.

Change one thing: keep on learning

If you cannot realistically see how you can change things at the moment, you can prepare for the future by gathering information, changing your attitude towards spending, and perhaps studying for a qualification. Instead of just waiting for the day to come when you will be magically free, think laterally about other ways you could satisfy your dream.

> You can prepare for the future by gathering information, changing your attitude towards spending, and perhaps studying for a qualification.

Lifestyle businesses often don't need start-up money

Gary used to work in a busy hairdressing salon, but he found the owner difficult and manipulative. He began dreading going to work and ended up taking time off with stress. He had always dreamed of owning his own salon, but as a single-parent of a teenager he found it difficult to save. He took further qualifications at his local college and this gave him the confidence to set up his own mobile hairdressing business.

His son helped him to set up a website and he had business cards and leaflets printed. He discussed everything with his son and they decided to be more careful with money. He opened a savings account and at the same time began hairdressing in clients' homes in his spare time. He waited until he had built up some regular customers before he resigned from his job.

One elderly customer moved into the local care home and, when he visited her there, he found himself inundated with requests from other residents. Gary says he always loved the work, but now he has the added bonus of being able to work the hours that he chooses. He is able to take days off during the week, spend more time with his son, and earn more working for himself than he did as an employee.

> "If you don't set goals for yourself, you are doomed to work to achieve the goals of someone else."
>
> *Brian Tracy*

Give it time

Thinking of and then launching a business is the exciting and easy bit – it is maintaining that initial energy and enthusiasm that is the true test.

The trick is to accept in advance that there will be setbacks – nothing ever runs smoothly from start to finish – and to admit that you will be tempted to give up when things go wrong.

> Accept in advance that there will be setbacks.

You have to give yourself a chance to succeed and remember that most new businesses do not make a profit in the first two years. Gary says that the one change he made, that gave him the confidence to leave his job, was to study for further qualifications. At the college, he met people with similar dreams and received valuable advice from his tutors. If you have done your homework and market research, you are much less likely to become discouraged if things don't immediately take off.

> "When I thought I couldn't go on, I forced myself to keep going. My success is based on persistence, not luck."
>
> *Estee Lauder*

Change one thing: ask for advice

My friend, Gill Hasson (co-author of *How to be Assertive*), became involved in a neighbourhood campaign to save a local church hall. In the process of fund-raising and advertising, she realized that there was no community magazine in the area. She decided to produce one, which would include the local community association's newsletter, articles from the local vicar and police officer, as well as from people running businesses in the area. She arranged a meeting with someone who already ran a similar magazine in a different location, and he kindly gave her lots of useful information about the cost of printing and how to get the magazine distributed.

She spent some time visiting local shops, vets, restaurants and galleries and got in touch with people who ran classes in the area. Although securing advertising was completely new to her, Gill soon built up a list of advertisers who wanted to advertise regularly in the magazine. She was able to start her magazine with almost no start-up costs.

She told me that she enjoys writing the editorial and articles, but there have also been unexpected benefits, such as getting to know her neighbours and the feeling of doing something useful for the community. She has also realized how many things were going on in the area that she didn't know about, and has joined a singing group after taking an advert for it for the magazine. She says that the one change she made was asking advice from someone who already ran a similar magazine. "That made the difference between just thinking about it and actually doing it."

"A business is successful to the extent that it provides a product or service that contributes to happiness in all of its forms."

Mihaly Csikszentmihalyi

If you don't have children, or they are grown-up, it is still a temptation to settle for the easy life instead of following your dreams. If you are in this situation, sometimes you just have to set a date and decide to do it. Daring to do something different, and perhaps adventurous, is life-changing and nothing ever looks the same again.

Making the decision

Leanne supported her family, in rural Cornwall, by becoming a painter and decorator. As soon as her children left school, they moved to Plymouth. Leanne had finished paying the mortgage on their small cottage, but she enjoyed living in a rural setting and was reluctant to move to the city.

She decided to spend a year travelling round the world (funded by renting out her cottage and selling her car). She met many inspirational people and she took the opportunity to think about what she really wanted to do with the rest of her life. She knew what she liked: being outdoors; being with other people; cooking and walking. By the end of the year, she had decided what she wanted to do. She raised money (by borrowing from friends and family) to build an extension (with some professional help) turning her home into a seven-bed guest house.

For the past 10 years, she has been hosting walking, drumming and creative-writing holidays from her home. She has also led walking holidays in Penzance and on the island of Gozo. She cooks all the food for their guests and often has to live in a caravan in the garden when the cottage is full. She says that travelling enabled her to think more clearly about what she wanted from life and how she wanted to spend it.

"Find a job you like and you add five days to every week."

H. Jackson Brown, Jnr

The devil is in the detail

The one change that Leanne made wasn't to move away or massively change her lifestyle. She analysed what she enjoyed doing best and thought of a way that she could make a living from it. She worked out exactly how much everything would cost; how much she could charge; how long it would take her to pay back the loan and how much money she needed to live on meanwhile.

Although you may have a general goal, such as "I want to run my own business", in order to succeed you have to be more specific: "I want to run a business selling organic vegetables". Then down to the details: "I'm going to have a market stall three times a week", or "I plan to sell door-to-door in my neighbour-hood". Then it is down to sourcing the vegetables and working out the running costs. Finding out what time you have to get up to visit the wholesale market and how much profit it is possible to make are a vital part of the planning – before you start.

Too many small businesses fall at the first hurdle because the person with the dream wasn't realistic about the effort needed and the financial gain to be made. You may need a timescale – if only to smile at in the future. But do write it all down – your end-goal and the steps you need to take to get there – this will free your mind from remembering and going over and over the same thing.

"If you talk about it, it is a dream. If you envision it, you gain excitement. If you plan it, it is possible. If you schedule it, it becomes reality."

Unknown

Change one thing: your attitude

Sometimes the change that you have to make is a change of attitude. Remember all those people in Chapter 1 who didn't regard age as a barrier to following their dreams? What do you think made them different from people who just settle into a routine and think that they have left it too late? Apart from good health, the main difference is simply attitude. All the people I have written about in this book have retained their enthusiasm and developed a positive attitude towards life. Use their stories as your inspiration: if they have done it why can't you?

Change one thing:
the way you think and speak

It is possible to change your thinking and to replace negative thoughts like "I'm not good enough" or "They'll never accept someone like me" with positive maxims like "I can do anything if I set my mind to it" or "I'm determined to do this however long it takes". If you change the way that you think and speak so that you begin your sentences with "I will . . ." or "I can . . ." instead of "I should . . ." or "I ought to . . .", your outlook on life will change and you will feel empowered instead of helpless.

What if your dream is to travel more?

In Chapter 2, we saw that the main regret of many people was not having travelled enough. If this is one of the goals in your life, you need first of all to examine what you mean by "travel". You may mean you would just like more foreign holidays: swimming in the sea, lying by the pool, or simply staying in a country with reliably good weather for two weeks. Many people are prepared to work for the rest of the year, in jobs they don't particularly enjoy, to pay for a few weeks in paradise.

This is fine. If it fulfils your need to travel, then your aim is probably to live more frugally the rest of the year so that you can take as many holidays as possible (and to find a job with lots of holidays). But if your dream really is to "travel" – to see something of the world, to absorb the culture of another country, to understand the people and their way of life – then this will certainly involve a change in the way you think about your work and your lifestyle.

Be clear about what you want and why you want it

One of the reasons that people regret "not travelling more" is because the desire to travel is not made sufficiently explicit. If you are serious about achieving your dreams, you have to approach them in the same way as any other goal.

Ask yourself these questions:

- ☐ What is my motivation?
- ☐ Do I believe I can do this?
- ☐ Am I prepared to put in the time and the effort needed to achieve my goal?
- ☐ Do I need help (and if so where can I get it)?
- ☐ What exactly is my plan (and does it have a realistic time-frame)?
- ☐ What will I do when things go wrong?
- ☐ How am I going to make sure I stick to it?

Amber and Ben met at university and both qualified as teachers. They had two children very quickly and spent their school holidays camping and caravanning in England. Their dream was to see more of the world, but they were worried about disrupting their children's education.

After much research, they decided to apply to British International Schools in Europe, as they would also admit the children of teaching staff. They both got accepted at a school in Budapest and their daughter took the International Baccalaureate at the school before gaining a place at university. After five years, they have now gained new posts in Alicante and will begin a new adventure there.

"Stuff your eyes with wonder . . . See the world. It's more fantastic than any dream made or paid for in factories."

Ray Bradbury

Studying abroad

It is often a change in attitude that is needed first of all. Once Amber and Ben decided that working in a different country could be beneficial to their daughter's education, they were able to take that leap. The desire to travel or to experience living in a different country can be combined with studying and working. In 2011, 20,000 British students studied for their degree abroad and a similar number study at European universities as part of their degree. American, German and Dutch institutions, in particular, want to attract British students and their fees can be cheaper than British universities.

Students can also work abroad during the summer vacation: Camp America finds jobs for students in summer camps in State National Parks and STA travel (formerly BUNAC) has a "Work America" programme that finds work for full-time students (and in Australia and New Zealand). They also have a sports coaching programme in South Africa where volunteers work with underprivileged children in Port Elizabeth.

It takes courage to study, or work, abroad as you have to get used to different food, accommodation and language without being able to take trips home at the weekend. But email and Skype make it easier to stay in touch and the insights and sense of independence that you gain can be invaluable.

Change one thing:
stop seeing age as a barrier

When Bill took early retirement at the age of 61, he decided to follow his dream of volunteering in Tanzania with the Voluntary Service Overseas (which accepts volunteers from the age of 18 to 75). He felt guilty about leaving his elderly mother behind, but his sister encouraged him to go and said that he was only a flight away. He has been there two years now and last year his mother and sister flew out to visit him.

He says that it is something he dreamed of doing all his life, but that he had always been too wrapped up in his career to allow himself to think it was possible. Bill said his one change was to think positively about the rest of his life, instead of deciding to settle into safe retirement.

"Take your life in your own hands and what happens? A terrible thing: no one to blame."

Erica Jong

Keeping the dream alive

Tom and Sarah met when they were both 19 and working on a caravan and campsite in the South of France. Eventually, they ended up running the campsite for the owners, who were often away. When Sarah became pregnant, they moved back to England, got married, and brought up their family of three boys. Tom was a photographer and Sarah worked as a care assistant. They often went camping in France with their boys and talked fondly of their time running a campsite.

When their youngest son was about to leave for university, they realized that they were now free to follow their dream. They had already researched the sites in the area that they liked and visited them to see if there were any job vacancies. They were surprised at how eager the owners were to employ a middle-age British couple and were soon offered jobs. They waited until their son had completed his first year at university and then rented out their house for the summer and moved to France.

Have a picture

If your dream is to travel and see more of the world, keep *your* dream alive by having a photograph or picture of the places that you would like to visit on your fridge or your desk (use travel brochures). Don't leave it until it is too late: don't become one of those people in Chapter 2 who spent their later years regretting the things they didn't do.

"When you dance, your purpose is not to get to a certain place on the floor. It's to enjoy each step along the way."

Wayne Dyer

Change one thing:
keep the dream alive

Tom and Sarah realized the life they wanted to live would be much easier if they were fluent in French. And so they decided that one positive change they could make was to take conversational French evening classes together. They also said that it was learning the language that kept the dream alive and they were convinced that this was one of the reasons they were immediately offered a job.

If you have a dream that cannot immediately be fulfilled, think about what you can do meanwhile to work towards it. Learning the language of the country where you'd like to live seems an obvious step, but it is surprising how many people talk of working or moving abroad without trying to learn the language. Remember, it doesn't matter what you were like at school; it is possible to learn anything that you want to if you have the motivation.

> If you have a dream that cannot immediately be fulfilled think about what you can do meanwhile to work towards it.

Gap year

According to a survey, in 2011, by the Post Office Travel Insurance, over a quarter of over-55s are thinking of taking a gap year – compared with 19% of students. They found that fewer students were able to take a gap year because of the rising cost of university fees. The over-55s were usually people who had been able to retire early and had received a lump sum as part of their pension. Being able to fulfil a lifetime's dream when you are older means keeping healthy and keeping your dream alive.

Barbershop quartet

Jim was a pensioner who had enjoyed singing in a barbershop quartet for 15 years. His wife enjoyed going to watch him at the venues where they played – often for charity. Both of them wanted to see more of the world while they were still active, but they knew their limited funds wouldn't allow them to do so. Jim discovered that one of the quartet was giving lectures on ancient Greece on a cruise around the Mediterranean and so he applied to the same company, offering to set up choirs and singing groups on board.

The pay was minimal, but he and his wife got to go on a luxury cruise with full board. He was 65 and continued to work the cruise ships, two or three times a year, for the next five years. His wife used the opportunity to enjoy ballroom dancing and practise her card-playing, which she had given up years earlier because Jim wasn't interested. On the ship, she made friends and felt totally safe. She enjoyed not having to cook meals and clean the house and felt that she deserved this after a life of working hard and bringing up three children.

"Enthusiasm is the yeast that makes your hopes rise to the stars. Enthusiasm is the sparkle in your eyes, the swing in your gait, the grip of your hand, the irresistible surge of will and energy to execute your ideas."

Henry Ford

Compromise

Notice how many times following a dream means compromise and waiting for the right time. Being in a relationship means having to take the wishes and needs of the other person into account, and being part of a family means meeting the require-ments of each member of the family. Sometimes, it means putting the dream on hold. But it doesn't mean giving up. To keep your dream from disappearing, it is important to have a plan and to feel that you are working towards the point when the time is right.

"20 years from now you will be more disappointed by the things you didn't do than by the ones you did. So throw off the bowlines. Sail away from the safe harbour. Catch the trade winds in your sails. Explore. Dream. Discover."

Mark Twain

Implementation

Finding the time

"Dost thou love life? Then do not squander time, for that's the stuff life is made of."

Benjamin Franklin

By now, you may be feeling: "This is all very well, but how on earth am I going to find the time and energy to change my life, in the way I would like, when I don't even have the time to do everything I should be doing now?" The most common complaint I hear from adult students is: "I just don't have the time", even when it is something that they have said they desperately want to do. Leading a fulfilling life doesn't mean spending every spare second rushing around from one task to the next; it means having the time to do the things that fit in with your values and aspirations.

> Leading a fulfilling life doesn't mean spending ever spare second rushing around from one task to the next.

Ask yourself these questions:

- [ ] Do you find yourself always complaining that there are not enough hours in the day?
- [ ] Do you feel that you are always in a rush and never have time for the things that are really important?
- [ ] Do you long to have more sleep and yet even when you go to bed find yourself lying awake in the early hours?
- [ ] Do you feel that you are constantly trying to catch up and that your "to-do" list just gets longer and longer?
- [ ] Are you often late for appointments?
- [ ] Do you commit to too many things which you later regret?

If the answer to most of these questions is yes, and you would like to change, then you first need to step back and look at the reasons for your hectic schedule.

> "Don't say you don't have enough time. You have exactly the same number of hours per day that were given to Helen Keller, Pasteur, Michelangelo, Mother Teresa, Leonardo da Vinci, Thomas Jefferson, and Albert Einstein."
>
> *Life's Little Instruction Booklet*

Are you a workaholic?

Sometimes you can spend so much time working and in activities that enable you to work (like travel arrangements, sorting out childcare, body and hair maintenance, and buying clothes for work), you get to the point where you feel there isn't time to think about your life in a rational or analytical way. Life becomes a rush of fitting everything in and being exhausted all the time. You feel a responsibility to your work and to your family and to your friends and feel guilty if you fail to meet a deadline or to help your child with her schoolwork.

It is easy to lose perspective about your life when you are working so hard all the time just to keep up with everything. Being interested and excited about your work isn't the same as being a workaholic. A workaholic is someone who has let work overtake their life to the detriment of their personal life and interests. It means having to be busy all the time – although this is often ineffective as a workaholic likes to be in control and has trouble delegating or trusting other people to do the work as well as they can.

"I appreciate all the long hours you've been putting in. However, it's been brought to my attention that you don't work here."

"One of the symptoms of an approaching nervous breakdown is the belief that one's work is terribly important."

Bertrand Russell

The Bergen Work Addiction Scale

This scale was designed by psychologists at the University of Bergen in Norway and colleagues from Nottingham Trent University to assess whether someone is a workaholic.

Try the test: Score 1= Never; 2= Rarely; 3= Sometimes; 4= Often; 5= Always

- ☐ You think of how you can free up more time to work.
- ☐ You spend much more time working than initially intended.
- ☐ You work in order to reduce feelings of guilt, anxiety, helplessness and depression.
- ☐ You have been told by others to cut down on work but not listened to them.
- ☐ You become stressed if you are prohibited from working.
- ☐ You work so much that it has negatively influenced your health.

(A score of 4 or above for any of these questions indicates that you may be a workaholic or in danger of becoming one.)

Researchers tested 12,000 workers from 25 different kinds of industry and the survey reflects the core elements of any addiction. Reporting their findings in the

> *Scandinavian Journal of Psychology* (June 2012), they
> said that addiction to work is becoming an increasing
> problem because the boundaries between home and
> office were blurred. Technology, such as mobile
> phones, laptops and tablet computers, means it is
> easier to also work from home and even on the journey
> between home and work.

Workaholism is often called the "respectable" addiction because workaholics can always claim that they are just working hard for the good of the family. Strangely, some workaholics are guilty of procrastination, in that they can start tasks but work at them inefficiently, or keep at them for longer than necessary, or do things that aren't necessary and so end up spending far too long on any one task.

> "Being busy does not always mean real work. The object of all
> work is production or accomplishment and to either of these
> ends there must be forethought, system planning, intelligence
> and honest purpose, as well as perspiration. Seeming to do is
> not doing."
>
> *Thomas A. Edison*

Back-to-back meetings

People who say they have "back-to-back" meetings or that they don't have time to talk because they are "busy, busy, busy" may be harassed executives, managers, office workers, teachers – in fact, anyone who allows their work to take over their lives. These and similar phrases are often used to elicit sympathy and a certain degree of admiration about how stressed and overworked they are. There can be a perverse pride in being too busy to enjoy the everyday common courtesies of speaking to a neighbour, returning a phone call, remembering a birthday or simply having time to chat.

> You are so absorbed in what you are doing you feel a sense of peace and timelessness.

Being someone who is too busy all the time is almost the opposite of being in a state of "Flow" (as discussed in Chapter 2) where you are so absorbed in what you are doing you feel a sense of peace and timelessness. When you are engaged in doing something that you enjoy in this way, you feel a sense of purpose and fulfilment. Whereas the constant activity of someone who is always rushing from one thing to another makes it difficult to ever become fully engrossed in one task and to feel the sense of satisfaction that this brings.

"Beware of the barrenness of a busy life."

Socrates

Putting off doing things, and spending too long on tasks once you do start, have the same effect: you get stressed by the amount you have to do. Admitting that you do have a problem with managing your workload is the first step. But the next step is deciding that you do want to do something about it. Try some of the following suggestions, but be aware that you are not going to change overnight. All change needs persistence and constant checking that you are not slipping back into your old ways.

How to stop procrastinating

One way of making sure that you complete an unpleasant or time-consuming task that you have been putting off is to promise yourself a reward when you have done it. This must be something you want (like a cup of coffee) or looking at your emails. So if you don't do it, you go all day without a drink or accessing your emails (only look at your emails at a couple of set times a day – they are too distracting).

Set a time limit

If this doesn't work for you, try just deciding to work for 20 minutes. Set a kitchen timer if necessary. The thought that you are only going to have to work for a short time might just persuade you to get started – and it is the getting started that is difficult.

Change one thing: do it now

Is there a telephone call that you should have made? Or an email that is nagging at your conscience?

Why not put this book down and do it now?

Do you need a to-do list?

At certain times in your life you may have created to-do lists to stop yourself from being driven mad by the fear of forgetting to do the endless list of tasks that seem imperative. If you feel like this, then it's a good idea to write a list of tasks – either on a Sunday night for the week (or at the end of each day, if you feel you have too much on your mind). But make sure that you write down exactly what you have to do.

Be realistic about how long everything takes

For example, instead of putting: "wrap and post birthday present", it may be that you first have to buy the wrapping paper, or find the Sellotape, or that you need the address from someone else. All these preliminary tasks are what cause you to procrastinate – you can't actually complete the task on the list until you do these things first. And they all take time, so your list for the day is probably unrealistic because you haven't allowed sufficient time in the first place. It can make you feel depressed and hopeless.

If you have a short list of things that can be completed, you will feel good about yourself and even energized to move on to something that you have been putting off for a while. Usually, it's quickest to simply list them and then number them in order of priority. It is satisfying to cross them off as they are done, but don't fall into the trap of writing down routine tasks (if you need to do this, then create a system on your computer that simply recreates the same tasks each day).

> "Those who make the worst use of their time are the first to complain of its brevity."
>
> *Jean de La Bruyere*

In fact, if any task is going to take only a few minutes, don't write it down at all; just do it straightaway. Then look at your list and see if you can find at least two tasks that you can delegate. You have to give up control to do this (and it can be difficult if you are perfectionist), but you are trying to change and this means stopping doing some things you are in the habit of doing and being prepared to try new things. The result might not be the same, but who cares if the dishwasher is stacked badly or the meal isn't the one that you would have cooked – the aim is to lighten your load and you have to lighten up to do this.

Some people find it useful to make a list of things to be done that day with a separate list for longer-term projects. If you are a list-writing person, a regular review of your lists (weekly or monthly) is necessary so that you can feel a sense of satisfaction over all the tasks you have completed. Sometimes, a review of your to-do lists will also indicate what you have neglected (for example, celebrating birthdays, meeting up with friends, doing something with your partner, or going somewhere you have promised with your child).

> "What is important is seldom urgent and what is urgent is seldom important."
>
> *US President, Dwight D. Eisenhower*

The balancing act

When people talk about trying to get the "work-life balance" right, what they always mean is that work is taking up too much of their time. One of the causes of breakdown in the family is when both partners work, but one also takes care of the majority of the childcare and domestic work.

A survey by the University of Missouri of 160 couples (published in the *Journal of Family Issues*) found that couples were happier and stayed together longer when men pulled their weight with the chores at home. All the couples had been married an average of five years and had at least one child. About 40% of the women had full- or part-time jobs. The more wives perceived their husbands were engaged in routine tasks around the home, the better the relationship was for both partners.

The consequence of allowing work to dominate your life, and at the same time trying to maintain a home and care for a family, is that your health and sometimes your sanity are at risk. The effect is often for something to break – people walk out of their jobs, give up on their relationships, and ruin their health. When you never have time to make love, or even to feel passionate and loving, then life has become a treadmill, where you have lost sight of what is important. If you think this is where you are heading, then take a step back and give yourself time to think and to breathe.

> When you never have time to make love, or even to feel passionate and loving, then life has become a treadmill, where you have lost sight of what is important.

Having it all

This phrase was first used by Shirley Conran in 1976 and is now being revived by Sheryl Sandberg (chief operating officer of Facebook and mother of two children). In her book, *Lean In: Women, Work and the Will to Lead*, she says it's women's fault if they don't get the top jobs because they don't push themselves hard enough. She advises that women should put their careers first and the rest will sort itself out (and men must do 50% of the chores).

She says that she fits in a workout before arriving at her desk at 8am; arrives home in time for her children's bath and bedtime; and then returns to work on her laptop until 11pm. Of course, women have just as much right as men to "have it all", but they do have to make sure they don't turn into the men they always criticized. Having a workaholic as a parent affects the whole family – what's the point if you don't have time to relax and have fun together?

Even if you pay for full-time child care, someone still has to organize the meals and the laundry and the bath times and bedtimes. If you are a single parent, you probably have no choice about going back to work. But if there are two parents, it is usually preferable if one of you is the main carer while they are small (or you manage to share the childcare). Of course, it doesn't have to be the mother: many women are passionate about their careers and can't wait to get back to work, and it often makes sense for the dad to stay at home instead (although in 2012 there were only 6,000 more fathers looking after pre-schoolers full-time than there were 10 years ago, according to the Office for National Statistics).

There are now 1.4 million households in the UK where the woman earns more than the man; in the last 10 years, the number of stay-at-home mothers has dropped by 44,000. It is, however, usually women who work flexi-time or part-time and women who take time off when the child is sick (even though men have the same rights as women in these areas). For women to take Sandberg's advice that they should prioritize their careers, it seems obvious that their partners must take on 50% of the domestic chores and childcare.

The traditional model of parental roles belongs to a different era and would make it difficult for each of you to achieve personal fulfilment. But having a family means lots of talking and planning for the future to make sure that you are both fulfilled and the children feel safe, loved and happy. It may mean one of you putting your dreams on hold, or both of you working part-time, probably managing on less money, and certainly there needs to be total trust and belief in each other.

"Not every successful man is a good father. But every good father is a successful man."

R. Duvall

But not at the same time

Having it all has come to mean: having a successful career; a loving long-term partner, and a fulfilling sex life; happy well-adjusted children; good health; loyal friends and a fun social life; exotic holidays; creative hobbies and outdoor activities. The list is endless. It is possible for men and women to have all these. But if you have a family, there will be times in your life when it is not possible for you both to have all these things at the same time.

"Everything changed the day she figured out there was exactly enough time for the important things in life."

Brian Andreas

The government's "Measuring National Well Being Report" of 80,000 people, conducted by the Office for National Statistics, asked people (on a scale of 1 to 10) how happy they were with their lives and to what extent they felt that their lives were worthwhile. They discovered that married couples scored the highest for life satisfaction (7.7); next came cohabiting couples (7.5); followed by single people (7.3); widows (6.8) and divorced or separated (6.6). Having children didn't make any difference to happiness ratings, but those who had children did feel an increased sense of meaning and purpose in their lives as they scored higher on the "worthwhile" section.

Change one thing: be assertive

Often in relationships, people fall into a pattern of behaviour and they assume that what they are doing is fine with the other person. It can be difficult to communicate your frustration if everyone has become accustomed to the way things are. If you have been the person who always sorts out the childcare; or remembers to change the sheets; or the person everyone turns to at work when something needs doing urgently, then you have to be assertive to get other people to take responsibility. It's not easy but it is possible.

- Choose a time when you have a receptive, and preferably captive, audience (in the car can be good with children).
- Tell them that you have something serious to say that is causing you to feel anxious/stressed/angry/upset (or however you are feeling).
- Tell them what it is.
- Ask for their help – but give them a specific responsibility (I'd like you to strip the bed every Saturday morning).
- Get their agreement and thank them for it.
- Be prepared to remind them until it becomes a habit.
- Decide what you are going to do if it doesn't happen (but you don't have to tell them).

Want-to-do list

Instead of writing a to-do list each day, try writing a want-to-do list: things that you would like to do simply because you would enjoy doing them. (You can have a separate "must-do" list if there are other things that you need to remember to do.) Try this for a week. Compare the two lists and see how many things you manage to achieve on the "want-to-do list".

> Instead of writing a to-do list each day, try writing a want-to-do list: things that you would like to do simply because you would enjoy doing them.

Have a visual reminder
If you find that things on your "want-to-do" list never get ticked off, then write next to each one when you are going to do it. Put the list where you can see it. It's a good idea to have in front of you a visual reminder of things that you want to do (and inspirational quotations).

Our son lives in Boston, but phones home regularly at different times. I was always impressed by this wish to speak to us, for no particular reason. Then when we went to visit, I saw the explanation: his mother-in-law had bought him a mug which said on the side, "RING YOUR MOTHER". He said every time he made himself a coffee in that mug he rang home.

A survey of 2,000 parents by the children's drink company, Ribena, revealed that a third of those parents who managed to find time for their family still found it difficult to switch off from "work mode" when they got home. They said that they worried about all the jobs that had to be done in the house even while they were playing or talking to their children. Two-fifths of the parents surveyed felt that they were failing as parents during the week; a quarter said they struggled to find time for their children on an evening after work.

They found that most working parents spent six times longer on daily tasks, such as commuting, cooking, and household chores, than they did with their children (186 minutes on the chores compared with 30 minutes with their children).

"For disappearing acts, it's hard to beat what happens to the eight hours supposedly left after eight of sleep and eight of work."

Doug Larson

Look back on the past week
How many times did you fail to ring a friend? How many times did you actually go for that walk? How many times did you play with your child? How many times did you sit in your garden or in the park and just listen to the birdsong? How many times did you speak to a neighbour? How many times did you just sit and chat to someone? How many times did you get to read a book? How many times did you sit quietly alone, or listen to music?

How do you spend your time?

These two clocks represent how you spent the day yesterday. Fill them in by shading each section and writing how you spent your time. So shade in the hours you spent sleeping; the times when you prepared and ate meals; the time you were at work; the time you spent travelling; the time you spent getting ready (to go out or to go to bed); the time you spent watching television, or reading, or listening to music or on your computer; the time you spent with your family talking or playing.

If yesterday wasn't a typical day for you, then draw your own clocks; you could do one for every day of the week or for a weekday and a weekend. It is important that you fill them in retrospectively so that they are accurate.

What does this show about how you spend your time? Do you spend most days doing something you enjoy? Do you do something you enjoy most days?

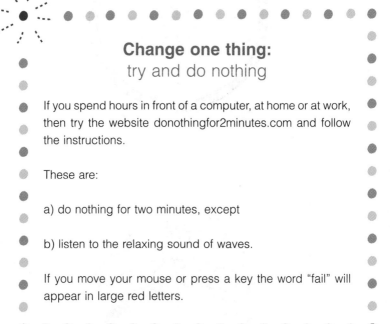

Change one thing:
try and do nothing

If you spend hours in front of a computer, at home or at work, then try the website donothingfor2minutes.com and follow the instructions.

These are:

a) do nothing for two minutes, except

b) listen to the relaxing sound of waves.

If you move your mouse or press a key the word "fail" will appear in large red letters.

Time is money

In the 2011 film "In Time" (starring Justin Timberlake and Amanda Seyfried), set in the year 2169, people can live forever as the "ageing gene" has been switched off. Instead, everyone has been genetically engineered to stop ageing at 25. From then onwards time starts counting down (literally a digital watch on the arm). So time becomes the currency: you can earn it, steal it or give it away (by simply pressing your arm to theirs).

In the film people live in different time zones according to their wealth (the amount of time they have stored) and die by running out of time. Those in the ghetto have to work long hours in the factories and the time they earn is barely enough to buy the necessities. In the wealthiest zone the inhabitants are immortal but have to have body guards because they are afraid of being mugged or murdered.

When the hero (Justin Timberlake) saves a suicidal man from being "time" robbed he gives him the 100 years he has left. Before dying he reveals that there is enough time for everyone to live a full life but the rich constantly raise the cost of living so the poor will always run out of time. It's an interesting idea (although it wasn't a box office hit): the rich have so much time on their hands they have to invent pastimes, like gambling (with time) and drinking. The poor never have time to enjoy themselves, or form proper relationships, because they are always working too hard just to make ends meet.

"How you spend your time is more important than how you spend your money. Money mistakes can be corrected, but time is gone forever."

Norris

Change one thing: learn to say "No"

Another reason that you become overwhelmed by the lack of time to do all those things that you really would like to do, is an inability to say no. You are allowing other people to set your agenda for the day if you find it difficult to say no to people who demand your time and attention. Every time the phone rings or someone stops you for a chat, you are permitting other people to take your time away from you.

Quite often, this is just another form of procrastination. You are allowing yourself to be distracted and to put off the things that you had planned to do. Or you might think, "I'll just look at my emails first", and then you answer some of them; before you know it an hour has gone by and you have not done the things you intended to do.

Be firm
If someone comes up to you when you are occupied and starts telling you something or says, "Can I have a minute?", have a ready response. Say something like: "Can it wait? I just need to finish this first". If you are afraid of appearing rude, then practise saying it kindly, with a smile. Then immediately go back to what you were doing.

At work
At work, if you find yourself always taking on too many commitments (which then become a cause of stress), ask

yourself why you do this. Often, it is because you like being needed: it makes you feel important when people ask you to do things (particularly when they imply you are the only one who can do it properly). Once the flattery, or cajoling, has worked, they move on and leave you to it. Or, sometimes, it is simply the desire to be liked: you don't want to upset anyone by saying no so end up saying yes to everything. The result is that your workload increases and you begin to feel resentful or inadequate because you can't cope.

With friends

You may have certain friends in your life that take up a disproportionate amount of your time. That's fine, if you don't mind. But if you have decided that you want to spend your time doing something else, then again you have to be brave and tell them: "I'm going to be really busy for the next few weeks. I'll ring you when I've got it all sorted." People can tell by your voice whether you mean it, or not, so again you might need to practise saying this in a firm (but not aggressive) manner. If you feel that you don't have time to spend with the people you like the most, then sometimes you have to weigh up how much time you spend socializing with people you don't really care about.

"Time is the coin of your life. It is the only coin you have, and only you can determine how it will be spent. Be careful lest you let other people spend it for you."

Carl Sandburg

When I teach assertiveness, many students say that they have a chronic inability to say no when they are asked to do something at work or socially. The technique is the same:

- If you are not sure, always ask for time to think about it.
- Check your body language and tone of voice (because you are nervous you may appear aggressive).
- Be polite but say the word "No" firmly.
- Don't give reasons or excuses (you can explain later, if necessary).
- Be prepared to compromise (after they have accepted your refusal).

True friends don't constantly demand your attention. In fact, your friends and the people with whom you spend most of the time will be a big influence on whether you are successful in your goals. The company you keep is a reflection of who you are: your closest friends and family can be the people who encourage you and keep you motivated; it is helpful to have them on board to share your excitement and enthusiasm.

Remember that the second biggest regret of the people in the survey quoted in Chapter 2 was: "Losing touch with friends". Some friendships can endure long periods of silence, but most friends need contact and affirmation that the friendship is important to you – make sure you keep the friends you do want.

> "The main problem with this great obsession with saving time is very simple: you can't save time. You can only spend it. But you can spend it wisely or foolishly."
>
> *Benjamin Hoff,* The Tao of Pooh

Emails

Dealing with emails at set times each day is a good time-saving tip, but you need willpower to do this. You can, however, train yourself to delete all spam without reading it and just flag the emails that aren't urgent, but need to be dealt with. If you have subscribed to companies in the past, unsubscribe as soon as you are no longer interested.

Change one thing:
avoid time-wasting activities

Start to notice what your own biggest time-wasters are: for some, it is spending too long on household chores. If you really want to spend time on a new venture, you have to learn to prioritize; to do things efficiently; delegate and let some things slide. If you have the money, paying a professional to clean or iron is a real time-saver. Think about what you pay to have done (such as clean your windows, or your car, or wash your hair) and work out which items are the greatest time-savers.

Other time-wasters may be switching on the television to watch a specific programme and then remaining glued to it. Much television watching is a mindless activity: it stops you having to think about anything else, because it is easier to stare at the screen in a kind of hypnotic trance. Similarly, reading magazines and every word of a newspaper can be a way of procrastinating and stopping you doing what you have decided you really want to do with your time.

Social networking sites can help you to stay in touch with friends and relatives, but only you can know how much time you "waste" on them. It is unlikely that one of your dying regrets will be that you wish you had spent more time on Facebook or Twitter.

Being late

Being late to work, to meetings, or when seeing friends, is a sign that you are not managing your time well. It is disrespectful towards the other person to keep them waiting: the hidden message is that your time is more important than theirs. If you are always in a rush, then you probably drive too quickly; miss buses and trains; lose things just before you set off and forget to take things that are important.

Change one thing: be early

You can change this behaviour and decide that in future you are always going to be early – not on time – early. Remember: everything takes longer than you think it will. Forget about trying to do all the things you usually do before you go out – just concentrate on being early to everything. Try this for a week and notice the feeling of relaxation and being in control it gives you.

Write: "BE EARLY" somewhere where you can see it every day; pat yourself on the back every time you achieve it, and check yourself every few weeks to make sure you haven't fallen back into your old ways.

Give your time away

Researchers at Wharton Business School in Pennsylvania discovered that helping someone else made people feel as if they had more time on their hands. They compared the effect of wasting time and giving time; they discovered that those who helped others, for a few minutes or a few hours, consistently felt as if they had more free time. It is counter-intuitive, but they concluded that giving away time in benevolent acts boosts an individual's sense of competence and efficiency. They said that your perception of how much time you have can change. So, in future, when you feel constrained by time, perhaps you should try to spare some time for others.

If your life is always too busy to do the things that you would like to do, then perhaps it is time to re-examine your priorities. Look at the list of values that you wrote in Chapter 2. Are you living your life according to these values? Always compromising your values means that it is difficult to be happy and to feel good about yourself. Time that you miss with your friends and family (but particularly your children) can never be reclaimed.

> "To love is to give one's time. We never give the impression that we care when we are in a hurry."
>
> *Paul Tournier*

Determination

Over to you

"Five frogs are sitting on a log.

Four decide to jump off.

How many are left?

Answer: Five.

Why?

Because there is a difference between deciding and doing."

Mark L. Feldman and
Michael F. Spratt

As you read this book, I suspect you will be have been tempted to miss out the exercises. You want to read on and find out what to do next. But change doesn't happen like this. There is no process of osmosis from the words on the page to your life.

You have to take things in stages, and the first stage is deciding what is important to you – what you are going to change. The next is to realize that it may be difficult and time-consuming, but that – if you have a plan – anything is possible. Acknowledge that there will be difficulties and drawbacks; the time will never be right and you will always have reasons to put things off and become discouraged.

> If you have a plan – anything is possible.

"Nothing will ever be attempted, if all possible objections must first be overcome."

Samuel Johnson

Be resilient

Being resilient means that you are prepared for setbacks and disappointments: you don't expect that it's going to be a smooth journey, but you have the reserves to enable you to persevere. You know that you can cope with anything and you are able to see setbacks as an opportunity to reflect and learn. Your goals are realistic and achievable, and you are not afraid to ask for help in reaching them. You maintain strong family ties and work hard to ensure that you are helping others to achieve their dreams too.

"Our greatest weakness lies in giving up. The most certain way to succeed is always to try just one more time."

Thomas Edison

Change one thing:
check your progress

Writing down your goals (as suggested in Chapter 5) is important, but it is also necessary to check regularly that you are working towards them. If you have made your aims specific and written dates next to them, don't become despondent if things happen more slowly than you anticipated.

One way of reducing risk is to take things slowly – just don't lose sight of your ultimate ambition. Keeping a diary, specifically for this purpose, is a good idea. You could use the online diary, OhLife.com, which is free and reminds you every evening to write something. It also shows you random earlier entries (and archives all your entries with easy retrieval).

You could use this as your "change" journal. So, for example, if the one change you have decided to make is to be early, you could record each day whether you achieved this. Once you feel happy that this has now become a habit (it could take months; it depends how long you have been in the habit of being late) you could move on to something else. By recording your achievements in this way, you will have an accessible reminder of how much you have changed. Remember: don't try to rush it or to change lots of things at the same time. Your mantra is: Change one thing.

"Only bad things happen quickly . . . Virtually all the happiness-producing processes in our lives take time, usually a long time: learning new things, changing old behaviours, building satisfying relationships, raising children. This is why patience and determination are among life's primary virtues."

Gordon Livingston

Look after yourself

It is difficult during a recession, when jobs are scarce and there is a lot of financial uncertainty, to think about personal fulfilment and change. Financial stability is a genuine worry, particularly if you have a family. But worrying doesn't stop things from happening. It is better to change your attitude towards spending money (buying endless consumer products that you don't really need) and to spend more time taking care of your health and well-being.

Taking care of your own health is all part of living a full and happy lifestyle. Believing that you are worth it means believing that you should look after yourself – with all the things you already know you need. Working hard, looking after a family, and having fun are all easier to achieve if you are feeling rested, well and energetic.

Not only will you find it difficult to accomplish your goals if you are exhausted and eating a bad diet, but you also won't get the same enjoyment from your lifestyle, however idyllic. Fresh air, exercise, nutritious food and a good night's sleep may sound like a simple prescription for good health, but sometimes you may need to check that these are integral to your lifestyle.

Staying young and enthusiastic in your outlook is much easier if you are feeling fit and well. Remember the healthy lifespan at the beginning of the book? Seven out of ten people in the health survey said that they thought their current lifestyle would have an impact on their quality of life as they got older. Imagine thinking this and doing nothing about it.

It doesn't matter what you have done in the past: decide now to look after yourself – you already know how. Don't just hope that you are one of the "lucky" ones who has a long healthy lifespan – make sure you are by living a rich and fulfilling life and taking good care of your body as well as your mind.

> "Don't let the fear of the time it will take to accomplish something stand in the way of you doing it. The time will pass anyway; we might just as well put that passing time to the best possible use."
>
> *Earl Nightingale*

Considering your own life and deliberating over the decisions that you have to make at turning points is all part of being human and leading a full life. You will never know how many years lie ahead of you, so it makes sense to make sure that you are not wasting them but that you spend your life in a way that makes you feel proud of yourself. The beginning is an important part of the journey, but dealing with obstacles and picking yourself up when you fall and keeping on are more important.

> The beginning is an important part of the journey, but dealing with obstacles and picking yourself up when you fall and keeping on are more important.

Be decisive but not impulsive

If you have young children or other responsibilities your career goals may take a back seat for a while. But not forever.

> Don't ever give up
> on your dreams and
> make sure that
> you are always working
> towards them.

Don't ever give up on your dreams and make sure that you are always working towards them.

All the people in the case studies in this book have suffered setbacks and difficulties while working towards their goals. Don't fall into the typical trap of drawing up a radical plan of action; trying to rush towards the end goal; expecting an immediate beneficial result and then becoming disheartened when this doesn't happen (this is why people don't stick to diets).

"It's never too late to be who you might have been."

George Eliot

Positive thinking

It makes sense to gather whatever help you can and to learn from the experiences of others before embarking on a potentially life-changing decision. Use the quotations to inspire you: choose your favourites, copy them out and keep them visible. When you feel positive about yourself and your expectations then you know that it is possible to move in the direction that you want to go and to achieve your goals. It is the way that you think about things that makes the difference: if you believe that you can make a change then you will. Commit yourself to taking that first step and the rest will follow.

> If you believe that
> you can make a change,
> then you will.

You too can be a self-actualizer

Only you can know what your dreams are and only you can decide whether you are going to fulfil them. Remember, Maslow believed it was possible for everyone to reach the pinnacle of the pyramid and to become a "self-actualizer". This means being the best person you can possibly be and there is no reason that you cannot achieve this.

> It is the way that you think about things that makes the difference.

If you see your life on this earth as temporary, if you want to live your life to the full, if want to look back on your life without any regrets, then you can. Others have done it. Why shouldn't you? This is your life and if you don't like the way it is going then change it. Nobody else can make this decision or tell you what to do. Once you take responsibility for your own life you give yourself the power to make the change.

> "The most difficult thing is the decision to act, the rest is mere tenacity. The fears are paper tigers. You can do anything you decide to do. You can act to change and control your life; and the procedure, the process, is its own reward."
>
> *Amelia Earhart*

You have to work towards your goal – nothing worthwhile happens overnight. When you have made this decision to make a change in your life, you will feel powerful, scared perhaps, but powerful – in that you are taking control of your own life instead of just letting things happen or seeing "how things turn out".

Remember that you just need to change one thing for your life to begin to improve. And, quite often, when you do make that change, the other things in your life that you want to change will follow. This doesn't necessarily have to be a huge change: even small changes in the way you behave towards others or how you look after yourself can make a difference. Many people find that when they begin to sort out things in their personal lives or their career then other problems diminish or even disappear.

Start now

The small steps that you can start now all lead the way to the lifestyle you deserve. Just feeling optimistic about the future, because you know where you are going and what you are going to do, can make a huge impact on your feeling of well-being.

"A year from now you will wish you had started today."

Karen Lamb

You can choose your own path. You can make the choice – instead of being led down a path or stumbling across it.

Take your life in your own hands and make sure that you enjoy being the person you always wanted to be.

Do something that will mean you have no regrets.

Do something that will make you feel proud of yourself.

Just remember: the first step is easy.

All you have to do is **Change One Thing**.

Acknowledgements

I am grateful to Ed Pringle and the staff at Royal Sussex Eye Hospital who saved my sight and inspired me to write this book. Thanks also to my friend and colleague, Gill Hasson, for being persistent and persuasive in her encouragement, and to my editors Jonathan Shipley and Jenny Ng for their wise guidance. I am indebted to my family and friends – and to all those who kindly allowed me to use their stories. And to Greg, for everything.

About the Author

Photo supplied with permission of Andrew Hasson

Sue Hadfield spent more than 20 years teaching English in comprehensive schools before beginning a portfolio career: university teaching, public speaking, coaching, and delivering workshops on career and personal development. Sue teaches assertiveness to teachers and managers and coaches children and adults on a one-to-one basis. You can contact her at www.makingsenseof.com.

Sue Hadfield is the author of *Brilliant Positive Thinking* and co-author of *How to be Assertive* and *Bounce: Use the Power of Resilience to Live the Life You Want*. After many years of procrastinating, she is now writing a novel.

Image List

IF YOU ARE

WAITING FOR

A SIGN,

THIS IS IT.